Dancing With Goddess

Deanne Quarrie

Edited by: Alexis Umowski
Cover Art: Drew Morton

All rights reserved. No part of this publication may be reproduced or transmitted in any form or by any means, electronic or mechanical, including photocopying, recording, or by any information storage and retrieval system without permission in writing from Deanne Quarrie.

Contents

Acknowledgements and Dedication	5
Introduction	9
Free and Bold	13
The Charge of the Goddess	15
The Goddess	17
What is Dianic Witchcraft?	19
Dancing the Year With Goddess	27
Tools of the Craft	33
Let's Get Started	43
The Elements Around Us	49
Creating Sacred Space	61
The Importance of Ritual	73
Energy Work	79
Sensing, Feeling, Moving in the Body	95
Living a Magical Life	109
Working With Crystals and Gemstones	129
Connecting With Our Kindred	135
Meditation	139
Welcoming a Goddess	147

Song and Chant	153
Collecting Women	159
Feminism, Politics and Spirituality	163
What to Do About Bullies	167
Healing the Wounds	173
Appendix	177
Suggested Reading	191
Bibliography	195

Acknowledgments and Dedication

I suppose it is quite common, when one sets out to write a book, that along with the desire to do that also comes all the unbidden thoughts our inner gremlins want us to hear. The sometimes-overwhelming fear that no one would ever want to read something you wrote. Or the question, "What can I write about that someone else hasn't already written?" Or even the most basic one of all, "What in the world would I even write about?"

These questions keep many of us from ever beginning the task. They are the questions, doubts and fears that harassed me for many years. Finally, about four years ago I decided that none of these questions were valid for me. They were just excuses. Not that there wasn't a possibility that they were valid, just that they were procrastinators and all that mattered was for me to get *it* out!

The hardest one was, "What would my book be about?" I think I was blinded because when it came to me, it was so obvious it made me laugh.

Anyone who knows me can tell you what my passion is. The Goddess and her Women are where (outside of making a living) all of my energies and love pour forth. It is as though there is no choice. Really, there is a choice, but what brings me joy is so connected to that which feels like the only choice—the one leading to a life filled with purpose. It is where my joy lives. It has come with sacrifice, I suppose, but the trade-off is worth it. I just know that those times I put it down, my life was just not "right."

When Goddess finally made sure I knew about Her, She did so with such swiftness that I was captured, ever in service to Her as Her priestess.

My first real teachers were those seeking growth who walked into Wikima (my now-closed bookstore). They showed me a need and so I set out to fill it. In the process, I gathered knowledge and teachings from any source I could find, so that I could then share it with them. The many public rites and rituals I was blessed to lead, and the festivals and gatherings I was a part of all contributed to an abundance of information and practice.

Then most loved of all, the circles of women who shared sacred space with me over the last 20 or so years; these have been my best teachers. They have blessed me with wisdom, laughter, joys and sorrows, always pushing me to learn and grow.

I wish to thank all of you, those who have moved on and those who remain. You have filled my cup beyond overflowing.

I wish to thank my children who put up with me when I experimented with burning all those herbs, making incense and stinking up the house; also for their encouragement and constant love, in spite of all the many mistakes I made. I offer gratitude to my daughter, Wendy, who was the first to hive as a priestess, blossoming into a beautiful, spontaneous, and creative high priestess making awesome magic in her own life. To Michael and Amy who grew into whole and healthy adults in spite of me, I give my loving thanks for helping their single Mom survive and for making me so proud. Then I was blessed with five grandchildren! It has been an interesting journey!

I wish to thank my friend, Pattalee Glass-Koentop, for allowing me the privilege of reading her manuscript for <u>Year of Moons, Season of Trees</u> before she ever submitted it to her publisher, initiating a life-long relationship with the Ogham and Her Sacred Trees. I miss you Pattalee! My thanks go to Mark Roberts, my good friend, for his beautiful words in our rituals.

I wish to thank Drew, my grandson for his incredible talent offered so generously for the cover art for this book.

My thanks also go to Alexis, a priestess in training in the Apple Branch, for her editing of this book.

I wish to thank those who left my Grove and Circle, sometimes in sadness or with disappointment; in spite of the difficulties during our time together, we all learned about living and loving.

Iris, Boudica, Brighid, Saffron, Kali Luna, Artemis de Lune, Lilitu, Sobeit, Malik Calliach, Mut Danu, Sorcha, and Ubastet, spiritually bound, mother and daughters, I love you.

I am grateful for the women who have given their hearts and energies to Global Goddess. It has taken pure dedication and love to be where we are today.

Dedication

This book is dedicated with love and gratitude to all the beautiful women whose hearts have touched mine; from The Ivy Girls to The Apple Branch, you are truly beautiful!

Introduction

So, Goddess has entered your life! This is a wondrous event and will be a magical adventure for you. Sometimes it seems She arrives in baffling ways or at the most inopportune times and yet, in retrospect, I can tell you, the timing is always perfect!

Everything fell in place for me at the age of 45 after a lifetime of searching and exploring, absorbing a little of this and a little of that until finally, with all that I knew, finally…I embraced Goddess.

I am not sure one "believes" in Goddess, at least not as I view Her. It comes down to actually "knowing" Her. I come from a very scientific perspective, always trying to blend what is fact and what is understood, sensed, or known from my own experience, and so for me, Goddess is a metaphor I have adopted as my own, a label of how I attempt to embrace what is sacred. I have always viewed the entire web of life as sacred, but never fully connected to the idea that I was fully part of that web or even understood my role within it until I allowed Goddess to enter me. While being a logical thinking woman, I was also a spiritual one, standing in awe of creation and the world around me. By embracing my personal concept of the sacred as Goddess, Her stories become my stories and help me in defining myself. Her faces are reflections of my own.

My walk with Goddess is self-defined by my own relationship with the Universe. Personally, I don't need labels as they have a tendency to box us in and I know that I am constantly evolving, but sometimes I need to use them, in hopes that others will understand something of who I am. For the purpose of defining myself to others, I call myself Dianic because I honor one Source and call Her Goddess. I call myself Witch because I have claimed my power and accept responsibility for crafting my own life experience. I call myself a Feminist because I am part of the solution to end sexism, sexist exploitation, and oppression.

This book is not just about Goddess. One can embrace a spiritual path based on a feminine divine and not practice magic or define themselves as a witch. That said, this book is about witchcraft that revolves around Goddess at the center of its practice. This book offers my own particular mix of modern feminine witchcraft blended with a somewhat-traditional path structured around the Ogham teachings. Combining the two has given me a freedom of creativity that is contained within a vessel of ancient wisdom.

I have been working with women, priestessing to their needs, for over twenty years. Occasionally, a woman comes to me wishing to be of service to others, looking for a guide on her path as a priestess. Working with these women has provided hope and beauty to my life, for through the years I have gained much from sharing in their dedication and singleness of purpose. I am most grateful to those women for being such inspirations for me.

What I hope this book will be is a tool to help you craft a relationship with Goddess and all that She is, as well as a means to develop your own personal magical path. There are many ways to get there. My way is not the only way. It is my hope that in your reading here will help you grow closer to defining your own view of Goddess and your place in the Universe.

Your Dance with Her began a long time ago. She lives in your memories and is now awakening you to the rhythms of Her Dance. Enjoy the adventure!

Free and Bold

Try to imagine, see if you can envision the beautiful Amazon women working together in love and trust, honoring their Goddess, provider of all. They are strong just as you are; calling on the support of their Sisters when needed, each woman knowing that the others are there for her if she should need them.

These women are wild women, meaning they are free spirits—connected in all ways with their environment—in tune with the energies about them, in tune with their own energies, unafraid and bold in how they live their lives. They stand up for those who suffered at the hands of outsiders, they fight for what is right, they speak the truth, directly and with courage and demand that they be heard.
They use the healing energy provided by the universe to heal themselves and others. They love freely, without jealousy, capturing the joy of every moment. All that they create with their hands or from within their own bodies is nurtured and loved. Their children prosper and grow healthy and strong because they are loved unconditionally.

This is your birthright—to live freely and without fear. You cling to what you know is right in your heart. You trust that you will always have what you need. You allow yourself to be vulnerable and open to love. You dance with the wind, revel in the warmth of the sun, and play like a child in the rain.

You are these Amazon Women, now, in this place, in this time, wild and free, strong and beautiful!

The Charge of the Goddess

Whenever ye have need of anything, once in the month, and better it be when the moon is full, then shall ye assemble in some secret place and adore the spirit of She, who is Queen of all witches. There shall ye assemble, ye who are fain to learn all sorcery, yet have not won its deepest secrets; to these will She teach things that are yet unknown. And ye shall be free from slavery; and as a sign that ye be really free, ye shall be naked in your rites; and ye shall dance, sing, feast, make music and love, all in Her praise. For Her's is the ecstasy of the spirit, and Her's also is joy on earth; for Her law is love unto all beings. Keep pure your highest ideal; strive ever towards it; let naught stop you or turn you aside. For Her's is the secret door which opens upon the land of youth and Her's is the cup of wine of life, and the cauldron of Cerridwen, which is the Holy Grail of immortality. She is the gracious Goddess, who gives the gift of joy unto the heart of man. Upon earth, She gave the knowledge of the spirit eternal; and beyond death, She gives peace and freedom, and reunion with those who have gone before. Nor does She demand sacrifice, for behold, She is the mother of all living, and Her love is poured out upon the earth.

She who is the beauty of the green earth, and the white moon among the stars, and the mystery of the waters, and the desire of the heart of man, calls unto thy soul. Arise, and come unto Her. For She is the soul of nature, who gives life to the universe. from Her all things proceed, and unto Her all things must return;

and before Her face, beloved of gods and men, let thine innermost divine self be enfolded in the rapture of the infinite. Let Her worship be within the heart that rejoiceth; for behold, all acts of love and pleasure are Her rituals. And therefore let there be beauty and strength, power and compassion, honor and humility, mirth and reverence within you. And thou who thinkest to seek Her, know thy seeking and yearning shall avail thee not unless thou knowest the mystery; that if that which thou seekest thou findest not within thee, then thou wilt never find it without thee. For behold, She has been with thee from the beginning; and She is that which is attained at the end of desire.

Originally written and published by Doreen Valiente.

The Goddess

Imagine living in a world that calls to a Divine Mother. Imagine being created in Her image. Imagine that because you are of Her, you are Goddess. Imagine Her pendulous Breasts offering nourishment for all. Imagine Her wide gaping Vulva pushing forth all of creation. Imagine Her generous Heart loving all that She has created with compassion and mercy. Imagine the fierceness of that same Mother, should harm or peril come near. Imagine a Mother who loves all of her children equally regardless of gender, color, social standing, sexual orientation, academic or financial worth.

The Goddess is the "All of Creation". She is both the Creatress and the Created. She is the Life Force of All There Is. She is all Energy. She is all Space. She is One, Whole, and Complete. Before Her, Nothing was. She arose from the Great Void, the Sacred Space of All Potential, giving Birth to Herself, before anything else had ever been born. She separated the Sky and the Water, and She Danced. In the Ecstasy of Her Dance did She conceive of All There Is.

In every culture, in every part of the world the Goddess was once revered as the Birth Giver of all Life. From the very beginning of time, in our earliest primitive state, we sought to explain the unexplainable by drawing from what we knew. The female of every species brought forth life, therefore the Goddess had also to be a birth-giving Mother, and the Great Mother was given Her identity.

She has been loved, feared, respected, honored, and glorified in every way imaginable throughout thousands of years of human development. She has been given a "face" for every conceivable aspect of Her nature. She has taken the form of animals, humans, and elemental energies. She has been given associations with plants, colors, sounds, stones, music, and more. For every aspect and every view She has a face.

She awaits you now. Take my hand; come in love and most of all, with joy in your heart.

Questions to ask yourself and suggestions for things to do:

How has your idea of the Divine evolved and changed throughout your life?

What events or changes in your life precipitated your exploration into the question of what is the Divine?

How do you perceive the Sacred in your life? How do you define The Goddess?

Take the time to journal your responses to these questions. Other questions may arise. White them down in your journal as well as thoughts and/or responses to them.

What is Dianic Witchcraft?

For every woman who calls herself Dianic, you will receive a different response to that question. Rather than quote other sources, let me just create for you who we are.

We are a Goddess-centered, earth-based, feminist denomination of the Wiccan religion revived and inspired by Goddess loving witches everywhere. In addition, we find tremendous value in a structure founded on ancient teachings learned from our kindred on the web of life, and material which comes from Druidic sources and The Ogham, Her Sacred Alphabet.

Our beliefs include:

- Belief in female divinity, who we call "Goddess."
- Celebration of eight solar celebrations and thirteen lunar cycles.
- A solid foundation of feminist ideology.
- A belief in the sacredness of our bodies.
- An understanding that the patriarchy we live in does not accurately reflect authentic experience.
- The basic beliefs of Dianics are shared by most Wiccans.
- Belief in the Wiccan Rede.
- We hold the principle of cause and effect as a foundational principle.
- We celebrate the holiday's common to Wiccans."

Mark Roberts and Morgan McFarland created a mixed-gender tradition that also identifies as Dianic and is

Goddess based. At its inception, it was simply called "Dianic, but in 1999 the name McFarland Dianic was adopted. Their rituals and practices are focused on the Ogham teachings and do not include Women's Mysteries. They do, however, honor Woman as Sacred as unto the Goddess.

Much of our tradition originated in the material handed down to me from themas well as from Mark's Faerie Faith. However, it has been adapted and expanded, as we believe nothing in life is static.

There are many who identify as Dianic. You will find quite a list at Witches Voice on the Internet. (www.witchvox.com) There is no one Way. There is no right Way.

The Apple Branch is a tradition within Dianic Witchcraft. Within our women only circle, we honor our Women's Mysteries as well as the seasons and cycles of the Sun, Earth, and Moon. We, as women, require our woman only space in which to heal and come into our own fullness. Both men and women have grown up in and are living in a patriarchal society. We have been taught both overtly and subvertly, behavior patterns that apply to how we interact with each other. The true value of woman only space is that it gives women a venue to just "be" - to be themselves, without the role playing inherent in our interaction with the opposite gender. Isolate us from those gender roles and we are more able to tap into our authenticity. By looking into the eyes of our Sisters and seeing Goddess and reflections of our selves, we strip away those societal norms and come to our true nature and find our Sacred Center. It is a healing we can find nowhere else as spiritual beings. It also serves as an authentic support system giving us much needed affirmation, energy and love. Regardless of spiritual beliefs and practices, women, in time honored tradition have always come together in woman only space for the sharing and telling of our stories. We have come together to honor the Mysteries of our bodies in ways that only women can fully appreciate. As women, it is imperative to reclaim our bodies as sacred. As women it is imperative that we reclaim our personal power and work together to overcome thousands of years of oppression.

We understand that we do not live in a world made up of women only and know that our relationships are critical to our lives. We take time to honor our friends and family by coming together where men, women, children are all welcome. In these Rites, we make no separation as to gender, age, or sexual identity. This is our family, or Clan. We come together at such times to celebrate the Sabbats of the Year or other life events where we would wish to share with all. These are our family gatherings.

In my heart of hearts, I choose to believe that there is much beauty in both men and women and that all are of Goddess. Our conditioning and ways of being, for both, have been twisted and formed, and shaped by the patriarchy in which we live. But deep within the core, both are beautiful.

We already know that those difficulties in relationships do not seem to be associated with the sex of the parties. The same difficulties arise with same sex and opposite sex unions. We both have so much to learn and one day I trust we will all be learning how to be together in harmony.

I chose women only space for my deep work with Goddess because that is where I can open and be true to my most holy center. I chose that arena to offer myself in service to women around the world. I could just as easily have stayed in mixed gender groups. However, as my love for Goddess grew, I knew that my work had to be with Her women. It is in this sacred space that we create together, that we women become whole, trusting, and healed.

Ultimately however, for most women it is critical that we then take this whole and divine woman back out into the world where men and women need to learn to be together in healing and trusting ways. We will always need and return to our woman only space for replenishment.

There is inherently something very special and unique in women's magic. Women's Mysteries belong to women and are held sacred in women only space.

To be Dianic is to be empowered by the Goddess in all that is. We know that time moves in a never-ending spiral of energy and love. We see the Mother's face in the world all around us, in the Original Earth Mother, in the wild, independent Virgin Goddess, Artemis, in the wildness of Kali Ma, and in the darkness of our Blessed Hekat.

We see the Earth, she who birthed and nourishes us, as female. We revel in all aspects of life on the planet and feel unbounding joy in living this life. We honor Her as our Mother. She is wise, ancient, full of deep mysteries and ultimately, unknowable. We honor Her as the womb of life. We also respect her as immensely complex and constantly engaged in acts of creation and destruction.

We call ourselves Witches. We practice magic. We are co-creators of our lives. We honor what is often called the "three-fold law." We recognize that everything we do has an effect. Much like the small stone thrown in a pool – the ripples go on and on and on...

Structurally, we are non-hierarchical. We come to our Circles with many diverse strengths and weaknesses. Each voice counts, every voice heard. We use consensus building as a part of our decision-making practice.

We honor two levels of service within our tradition, that of Priestess and that of High Priestess. From the Branch is the educational arm of the Tradition where we all learn and grow together in Goddess.

We meet in groves and covens and our work is as inclusive of all present as possible. The High Priestess functions as Ritualist, Guide, and Mentor for the group. She may work with a priestess-in-training (sometimes called the Maiden) or she may work at the altar alone. We have Covens who meet in person and those that meet in cyber-space.

What about men in Circle? Is it not possible that men can be called to honor the Goddess? How wonderful for them to find community that offers opportunity as co-creators in a non-threatening environment to explore who they are, a place that is both non-competitive and non-hierarchical where they can stand in awe of the universe and learn to work in harmony, removing stereotypical and archetypal responses to that interaction. Why could they not find a place of deep personal connection with Goddess and experience a healing and joyous homecoming? I believe it would be foolish to think that those things that brought me to the Goddess would not also call to her sons. While we do work our Lunar Rites as women only Circles, our tradition does offer an open and loving place for men at our celebratory Sabbat Rites. We have our women only solar passages, as well, but also provide sacred space for the coming together of families in joyous celebration. We honor life passages for all members of the human family. Through our work alone and in our coming together, we are creating new and better ways to live and grow together in Goddess.

I am often asked about the question of duality, as a matter of balance. I am told all the time by traditional Wiccans that one must honor both Goddess and God as reflective of the ways of nature where all things are balanced as female and male, that as a Dianic, I am not in balance. But you see, Dianics perceive energy differently. We find the idea of "male and female energy" uncomfortable and limiting, and also impossible to define. We view Goddess as Whole, containing all. We also view ourselves as Whole, containing All. I do not need someone, outside of myself to be whole. I do not need another to provide balance in my life. I know that I am a blending of all energies, and balanced, just as I am. I question the beliefs of Carl Jung that teach that inside of every woman is a male side or that inside of every man there is a female side. Because I am a woman, all that I am is female.

Our concept of energy comes to us by observing the world around us, for in reality all of life is energy. Energy is in the tides or the ocean and in the cyclical seasons of the year. We see and feel energy in our Circles and see how it flows in the Spiral. Energy surges and retreats again and again. We observe it in our cycles of birth, growth, death and rebirth. We watch it in the in the phases of the moon and in the stars. We don't see everything as linear, but rather view life as a spiral. We look at everything around us. We look at the trees and mountains, at the stars and the clouds, the seas and rivers, the sun and the moon. In them is the pulsing music of the One Force that not only runs the Universe, but IS the Universe. Dianics name it Goddess and honor it as feminine, as Birth Giver. The Goddess is love, honor, and power. She is forceful and She is yielding. Order and Chaos are Hers. She both turns the Wheel and is turned by it.

Questions to ask yourself and suggestions for things to do:

How do you feeling about what you have just read? Write in your journal any thoughts, feelings, or perceptions that arise in your reading.

Do you have questions about anything you have read? Examine how you feel? What is your reaction to the word witch? Witchcraft? What about practicing magic? Do the words alarm you? Do you feel good when you think the words? What if you say them out loud?

How do you feel about women working alone in Circle? And how do you feel about men and women working together in Circle? Do you see a need for both? Spend time writing in your journal any thoughts feelings, questions that come up. Each of us needs to have our own personal concepts and identification, our own truths that resonate for us, in a very personal way.

Recognize that these truths can change, grow, expand, and diverge in many different directions over time. No right, no wrong – what is important is that your own truths help you, serve you, and bring you joy and fulfillment in your life.

Dancing the Year with Goddess

When a person begins to dance with Goddess it is a natural progression to begin to live by the seasons of the sun and moon. It just makes sense to create a foundation of our spiritual practice on observable patterns of our Universe. We can observe that the Moon travels in a predictable orbit around the Earth, being seen in our sky beginning with a new crescent of light enlarging to full and finally disappearing only to return again to repeat the cycle. We have many options available to us to honor these cycles, working in harmony with the progression of the Moon around the Earth. The next observable cycle is our own Earth's rotation around the Sun as we move from the Dark of Winter into the Fullness of Summer and then, just as with the Moon, we return once more to the Dark. Honoring each of the Seasons keeps us in rhythm with Her many faces as we move through the year. Not only can we celebrate the seasons of the agricultural year, but we can also honor them by celebrating the seasons and cycles of Woman.

Most of us are very aware of the Solstices and Equinoxes, when they occur and what is happening with the Sun and the Earth at those times. If not it will be explained later in this chapter. There are four times that the ancient people of Europe got together to celebrate, and these holidays are referred to as the Cross-Quarters because they fall in between the Equinoxes and Solstices. The occasions they marked themselves were honored even more. I use the names for these holidays as I learned them but I will share alternate names as well. I will travel through the year with the following descriptions and include Cross-Quarter Days, Solstices, and Equinoxes.

Samhain honors our Ancestors, the Beloved Dead, the Old Ones, and the Goddess in Her aspect as Crone. The Crone joins us in rites, as do the Ancestors and the Old Ones, offering light on their journey as they travel to us. We know this today as Halloween. It is also called Hallowmas or Hallows, All Souls and All Saints Day. This is the point at which the last harvest occurs, that of the livestock, and this is the true entry into the "dark" of the year.

Next is the celebration of Winter Solstice, which is also known as Yule and Mid-Winter. It marks the rebirth of the sun and is a festival of giving and receiving gifts, filled with dancing and singing. The Goddess manifests as the Hag who carries the inner fire of rebirth from deep within. We often refer to Her as "Seed inside Hag."

Next is Imbolc or Candlemas, which marks the beginning of Spring. We make Brighid wheels, make and bless the new candles for the year and give each other new brooms. We might prepare a special bed for Brighid and invite her to bless the gifts. We eat special breads in honor of the Grain Goddess. We spread a cloth (called Brid's mantle) on the ground to catch the first spring dew. This is also the traditional time for initiations and dedications.

Next follows Ostara, the Spring or Vernal Equinox, sacred to Eostre. We dye eggs and exchange them. The White Hare brings baskets of candy to the children. We balance an egg on its end, celebrating the time of equal night and day. We include play in our rites, honoring the child within. We turn the Wheel by planting seeds into the stirring soil to germinate our growth.

Next is Beltane, a time of creativity and fertility. We decorate the Maypole and dance, as well as taking the time for cleaning and freshening-up our altars. Our ritual includes a fire, which we jump, with a lot of singing and shouting. It is the beginning of Summer and we delight in the coming long warm days. We honor a young woman's first blood and as adult women, we remember our own first bloods, reclaiming our pride and heritage as Women, honoring our life-giving bodies.

Midsummer, the Summer Solstice, finds us feasting and celebrating on the longest day and shortest night. Our ritual honors the fertility of the Mother and all Her bounty. We light fires and dance and drum until dawn. This is a time of sexual pleasure, and laughing and feasting are all part of the dance. And finally, our rituals include gratitude with the exuberance of the season.

At Lughnasadh or Lammas, we gather the summer vegetables and fruit from our gardens. We honor them as the First Fruits of the Harvest. We look at our harvest and the harvest that is still to come. We acknowledge the sacrifice made toward our bounty. This time is set aside to honor the peri-menopausal woman—her children are grown and she is at the peak of her creative abilities. She is a strong and proud woman, free and ready to explore her power and ability to give to the world.

At Mabon, the Fall Equinox, we honor the Goddess in her aspect as the Coming Crone. We celebrate a second harvest and acknowledge the balance of dark and light recognizing that this is the beginning of the darkening of the year. We offer thanksgiving for the year that is rapidly passing and offer back some act of service or commitment to make life better for the Whole. We dance a spiral dance and begin the deep dreaming and divination of the approaching dark times.

At Samhain we return once more to complete and begin, death and birth, the ever turning Wheel of the Year.

We affirm that life in all its mystery is sacred. We make every effort to be fully mindful of the Law of Return. We believe it is important to take responsibility for our actions as well as our reactions. Because it is difficult for us to separate our spiritual life from our political one, we are active in political activities, especially on any issue, dealing with oppression or which affects freedom of religion as well as the environment.

We believe in rearing our children in our spirituality as well as teaching them of other paths and we honor their life transitions in rituals just as we do for the adults. Following the birth of a new member of our clan-family, we hold a ritual called a Welcoming in which the child is presented to the Goddess, to the Ancestors, to the Old Ones, to the Spirits of the Land, and to the clan-family. When our children reach puberty, we ritualize the moment with the First Blood Rites for girls and Greening for boys. We unite persons in love through a Hand Fasting. We mark Eldering through Croning and Saging rituals. And we bid our Beloved Dead farewell with a service of the Rites of Crossing. We do other life passage rituals as they arise. A woman whose children have left home might need a special celebration. A family member who has lost a job may need the support of the family. A new home is blessed. Relationships that have ended are closed in sacred space, just as they began.

We rely heavily on the Mysteries as revealed in all of nature. We honor those Mysteries in our Lunar and Solar Rites. We honor thirteen lunar cycles within the year. Our Solar Rites honor our solar cycle, the Seasons of the Sun, as we, living on the Earth, travel around her. The Seasons are Her light waxing and waning upon us.

Tools of the Craft

Every religion I have ever looked into or studied has its own set of ritual tools. Most of these tools have come into being simply by their usefulness and have, though use, become visual symbols of the work they represent.

Pagans are no different and we as Dianic witches use most of these same tools as those described by other pagans.

What follows is a pretty complete list but should not be construed as complete and even in the definitions offered, you may have other uses or even different uses both in actual and in symbolic use. There will always be those tools and symbols that are specific to one's own personal path.

The most important aspect to realize about tools is to understand they are not absolutely necessary. The most important tools are your heart and mind. Your finger makes a great wand and an outstretched arm can cut as cleanly as a knife or sword in a ritual. Your cupped hands upraised for a chalice can add an element to a ritual that often the "real thing" cannot.

It is not necessary to spend your life savings on tools; in fact, those crafted by your own hands are most desirable.

What follows below is a list of tools and a brief explanation of each. Tools may be personal, as those used only by you and as "group" tools, which would be those, used by the whole coven.

First of all, your own sacred space, your Circle of Power, is as much a tool as anything you could buy from someone. As a primary tool, it provides the "container" for our work. It does not have to be elaborately laid out or be extravagant in any way. It can be created in your own mind in whatever creative way you can envision.

This leads us then to the altar. An altar is a nice way of projecting outward your feelings toward our Goddess and the different energies that make up life. Creating your own altar gives you a visual upon which to project your own ideas and concepts of the divine and/or to place other symbols representing the work you wish to do.

All ritual tools are used as a focus for concentration and visualization. You can imagine a flow of power coming form a wand. The symbolic meaning is deeply imprinted on the mind. Looking at them and using them helps visualization and in focusing the state of mind.

Pentacle - A pentacle is a circle with a five-pointed star in the center. It is usually made of silver, copper, bronze, or wood. It is circular and flat and is usually from 5 to 9 inches wide. This tool is associated to the element of Earth, and for us is placed in the North and represents Earth. The five points of the pentacle symbolize the five points of fellowship, and also the five elements (Earth, Air, Fire, Water, and Spirit). The pentacle represents the body and the physical. It represents strength, and is used to ward off negative energy.

Wand - The wand is usually made of wood and sometimes contains crystals and/or symbolic markings. But it can be made of anything you desire. It is nice if the wand should is made from the Sacred Trees. For some the wand represents the element of Fire and the direction of South, and for others it represents the Element of Air and is placed in the East. This is entirely personal preference and/or training. Traditionally it is the length of the users arm; from the tip of the practitioner's middle finger to elbow, preferably made from fallen wood.

It is a very personal tool that can be used to direct focused energy. It can also be used to call Quarters, and for a multitude of other purposes for which energy is channeled. Some pagans have two wands; one for Circle ritual work and another for spell work. One of these will most likely be charged to the type of work being performed, while the other is a "power wand." The Power Wand is usually handmade (or at least, finished) by the individual.

Candle - The candle, when used to represent the Element Fire, is placed in the South. Candles have many uses in ritual and magic – a huge topic written about in many books. We use candles on our altars to resent the Goddess, the Work of the Ritual – the members present, but there are many ways to use candles.

Athame - This is the witch's knife. Is typically said to be a black handled knife, but color really is not important. This is one of the four most important tools that you will need on your altar. It usually is double edged and is never used to cut anything except the air. Most people use this tool to physically cut open their circle. For some this tool is associated with Fire and placed in the South. To others it represents Air and is placed in the East. This is a matter of personal preference and/or training. It is considered by some to be very important that the ritual knife never be used to draw blood. However, some traditions do use it for just that – a drawing of blood to create a pact between one person and another.

Sword - The sword can be used in place of, or in addition to, the athame. Many groups who limit the use of the sword to just the Priestess; others will often bring their own swords to mark the boundaries or quarter points of the circle.

Incense Burner/Incense - Incense is associated with Air. Its scent and uses depend on the working being preformed. Also "censer" or "thurible"... A container used to contain a hot coal for burning incense. The incense itself represents the element of Air while the fire (charcoal) represents Fire. The combination of these two elements is used to purify ritual areas, other tools or the circle itself.

Crystals & Gemstones - Placed in working area. They symbolize Earth and North. Uses and types vary.

Cauldron - Associated with Water and West. A symbol of the womb, representing the female ability to contain and nurture. Also used to make brews, it can be filled with water and used for scrying. It is usually three legged representing the Triple Goddess and also bounty and blessings. It has also come to represent the concept of reincarnation and the cycles of birth, death and rebirth. Cauldrons can be used to represent water and used for scrying.

In the Apple Branch we use a cauldron in every ritual and teach our students all of the many variations of cauldron building.

Chalice - The chalice is a basically a cup which should contain water. However, it is much more then that. The chalice is the main tool that represents the element of Water and the direction of West. It is most often placed in the Western quarter of your circle, and can contain a liquid of your choice. I use only water in mine representing the Goddess as Giver of Life. For me it represents the female womb, and symbolically is represents the realm of feeling. It is associated to the Mother, and also the moon. It is used in our Circles to offer libations and blessings.

Boline - The Boline is used for cutting herbs and other practical purposes. It is usually a white handled knife. This is the Healer's Knife, used for cutting herbs and preparing and stirring herbal potions and medicines. It is allied with Earth. As with the athame, a regular kitchen knife, set aside so that it never touched blood, was often used as a Boline during the Burning Times.

My boline is small, has a curved blade and the handle is made from the tooth of a hippopotamus.

Besom - The Besom is the Witches Broom. It is used to ritually cleanse the working area. I personally use mine in workings where I need to remove anything from my life – I sweep it away. I clean my sacred space and sometimes do my whole house that way! I also sweep any negativity I find right out the door!

Ritual Workbook/Book of Shadows - A Book of Shadows is a book of the philosophy of ritual, and perhaps rituals themselves. The BOS rather than being a Grimoire, is more like your own personal magical diary. It holds not only spells, but can also include Sabbat rituals, elemental/astrological/deity correspondences, as well as any of your writings of magical work, especially the results and consequences (both good and bad!). Though written by hand in days of old, the traditional black leather-bound book of Shadows is quickly giving way to Electronic versions. Just remember to have a hard copy close at hand so you don't lose everything when your hard drive crashes!

After all these years, I am still unclear as to what the difference is between a Book of Shadows and a Grimoire. I keep only a Book of Shadows.

Drums and other percussion instruments - These are used to make music during certain ceremonies and rituals. Often used to induce a trance state. I enjoy the use of all kinds of music in my rituals – drumming is a marvelous way to raise power as is singing.

Mirror - Used for scrying, is usually black-backed.

Necklace - These can be made on, or for Initiation day in some Wiccan covens. In others they are given as a symbol of completion. They are used in some rituals, worn often and during every Esbat for perfection and power. Also can be ritual amulets, etc. The Apple Branch has a special one only for high priestesses.

Bowl of Water - Placed on the altar to represent the Water Element. Often used for scrying.

Bowl of Salt - For protection, also sprinkled around the circle to purify it.

Bell - Sometimes used during ritual, they are associated with the divine: their sound is symbolic of creative power, their shape a symbol of the female force. Most often to open, setting the tone, and also used to close, to bring the focus back to now time.

Staff - Used to mark quarter points or as a "stang" to hold banners representing elements or other unique symbolic flags. Very often the witch's staff is her symbol of her own personal power upon which she may hang her own personal symbols. I have not sued mine in ritual very often but when I do it almost feels as though I am making a statement – "This is my space, and I claim it as my place of Power."

Measure - The Measure is a length of cord, cut to your exact height, plus other measurements, during a coven initiation. This is also called a cingulum. In traditional Wicca, the Measure is often kept by the High Priestess in order to assure everyone's secrecy regarding the group. If a member of the group betrays the group, it can be used to bind - to silence the offending member. When a member petitions the High Priestess to leave the group for whatever reason, the Measure was burned once she gave recognition and blessing to the change. Since we no longer live with such dire need of secrecy today, some modern groups give the Measure back to the initiate as a symbol of love and trust. Some of these pagans then add a knot to the cingulum for each year a day they've been with the group, and wear this as a belt during Circle rites.

The Mark - A piece of parchment paper used to collect the blood of the initiate in many Wiccan covens. This paper can be held by the High Priestess to be used against that member should they break oaths made to the Coven. Many modern covens still practice this and any woman entering a coven needs to know this in advance if at all possible. At this time in my life, I would not wish to participate in any group who would hold a part of me "in case." I believe in the words "love and trust" and prefer a demonstration of such.

Ritual Robes - The mode of dress for most groups is generally robes, but this is not a hard and fast rule. Some groups wear a mix of robes and clothing from the medieval or renaissance period. Some groups hold fast to the custom of being skyclad in their rites. Whatever is worn (or not worn), I believe it should be clothing that has been "set apart" from the mundane world and used only in ritual. It should be loose enough that movement is not impeded, but not so flowing as to be a danger around the cauldron and/or candles. Ritual jewelry is not necessary, but many have specific pieces they wear only at ritual. In addition, it is not unusual for the High Priestess to wear a circlet, tiara, or garter in symbolism of her position as representative of the Goddess during Circle Rites.

Magical/Goddess Name - One last "tool" that many may not see as a tool, is the name you choose upon initiating into the Craft. Care and consideration need to be observed when choosing a name, so that it reflects that which you are or strive to be at your innermost core. This can be accomplished in many ways, the best being during a dream walk where the Goddess, the Ancients, your totem, or your spirit allies give the name to you.

Let's Get Started

Looking at the Journey

Each of us has a personal spiritual journey. At special times in our lives we are touched or triggered by individuals and/or events in our lives that stop us for a moment, give us pause for thought, turn us ever so slightly on the path we walk. These are opportunities for personal growth whether we are aware of them or not; steps that induce a deeper search; a setback that gives us time to consider who we are or where we want to be.

It is important to know how you got here from there! It is important to understand what things happened in your life, what people you met, what those things were that influenced you in the decisions you made, and what caused a deepening awareness in yourself as a spiritual being.

One way that you can do this is to journal your life experience, marking transitions, naming events, people, places and things that influenced you spiritually. Try to get into detail; not just who, where, and what but why and how, as well.

For those more visually oriented it might help you to start with a timeline. There will be times in your life when many things happened and you may need one line just for one year and another line may cover a ten-year period. It is an interesting exercise. Once you have the visual, you can then journal the experiences.

Spend a few days on this project. Begin your journal now. Allow yourself time to reflect to dig deeply into your memory, searching for experiences, chance happenings, mentors, family members, anything or anyone who might have had an influence on your spiritual self.

Setting Goals for Yourself

It is very helpful to sit down and create a plan for yourself when you begin a project. Creating a plan for the development of self is no different. Without a plan we are tossed and turned by life, unaware of beginnings and endings, and dragged down by aimlessness and a feeling that life is headed nowhere.

When you set goals it is important that you be specific. Be very clear in deciding what it is you want. Be very exact. Write it down. Be sure you have a clear understanding of what you are setting out to do.

Make sure that you set up some system to outline your progress. I like to use the lunar cycles for the small steps and the Seasons of the Year for things needing a bit more time. Make absolutely sure that you truly can attain your goal with the time and resources you have available.

Be sure that your goal has a definite result.

Set a deadline for each part of your goal.

Neglect one of these guidelines and the odds drop in achieving your goals. Why?

The key force that either drives you towards your goals or holds you back is your subconscious mind. These goal-setting guidelines are necessary criteria for your subconscious mind to accept your goals and start working for you. Otherwise it will work hard to keep you in the comfort zone of your present conditions and old habits.

With a specific goal you can clearly see what it is you want to achieve, and you have specific standards for that achievement. In making your goals specific it is important that you actually write them, which is crucial in all goal-setting guidelines.

The more specific your goal, the more realistic your success will be.

When you work on making your goal specific, you program your subconscious mind to work for you. Then, your feelings and thoughts will lead you to your goal instead of pointing at the obstacles. To make your goals specific you also need to work out the other components of goal-setting guidelines below.

You need a way to measure the progress and some specific criteria that will tell you when you can stop and the goal is achieved. Feeling the progress is very important for you to stay motivated and enjoy the process of achieving the goal.

You must see a realistic path to achievement, and reasonable odds that you get there. This does not mean that the lower you aim the more likely you reach success. It is well known that goals that work best have a challenge in them. They are chosen as ambitious as possible, but still reachable. Then they will give you more motivation as well as a sense of achievement.

Your goal will be rewarding when you have clear reasons why you want to reach that goal. This is one more place where it is important that the goal is really yours. Have your specific reasons and expected reward in writing. If possible, even add some visual pictures.

Imagine how you are going to feel when the goal is finally reached. This will ensure that the goal is really worth achieving. Then, every time you get stuck and don't feel motivated enough, read your reasons and look at the pictures. This is a known and very powerful, practical technique of how to get through difficult moments without quitting.

The final requirement of these goal-setting guidelines is that your goal should have a specific time limit. This is also very important for your subconscious mind. Besides, time is the price you pay for the reward from achieving a goal. Setting the deadline will protect you from paying a higher price than the goal is worth. This is also your protection from either procrastination or perfectionism.

With all this in mind, take a bit of time now to set goals for yourself. How do you wish to use this book? How would you lay out a Year and a Day of study utilizing the tools at hand? What are your resources, what do you wish to achieve, how much time do you have available, and when can you plan to spend time each day for the work?

Spend time with your journal creating your goals and plans for the coming year.

Questions to ask yourself and suggestions for things to do:

If you have not already done so, begin a journal. Begin with your own personal spiritual journey. Record that journey. Tell your story.

Take a look at where you want to go on your walk with Goddess for a set amount of time. It could be for three months only, or you may wish to plan for your official Year and a Day of study.

By now you may have looked into Book Two and found your place on the wheel. Write down how you wish to use this book.

Plot each Lunar Cycle with how you wish to spend some time with Goddess and her lore. Write down areas you want to explore, when to do that, and how much time to spend on each. Know that you can change this plan at any time.

Record your thoughts and feelings about the beginning of this journey.

The Elements Around Us

Being ~ In Your Embrace

I feel your breath on my skin like the gentle wind blowing in my face as I open the window to my garden in the morning. I breathe your air, feeling it enter me. It becomes our breath, our clean, sweet air.

You surround me in vibrant color with red, yellow, purple, and blue wildflowers dancing at my feet. Sweet and pungent, your scent drifts toward me, warming me, reminding me of loves I have known. Memories of passion, each embrace a sacred moment with you.

Dew-fresh, I am called to gaze upon your beauty. I touch your sweet petals; they unfold, soft as velvet to my touch. I am renewed with your awakening.

My own heat rises as your sunlight streams upon me. With your energy pulsing through me I am transformed. Passion stirs in me. I am at once lifted, seeking and yearning for your embrace. Feeling my heart, beating to your rhythm, I am reminded of the joy in life.

Your Holy Waters bring forth life. Sweet gentle stream, I lay beside you in such pleasure. I dream of loss, renewal, and then, hope. I feel the life force of my womb, which once brought forth life. I recognize your flow in my blood, my woman's blood, now but a memory in this crone's body, still strong and sure.

Suddenly I am in all waters, first riding the wave of the ocean, reveling in the speed of my body moving with the wave, then in a cascading waterfall, which showers me in newness.

I lie on the ground and feel you, Mother. Your cool, damp soil runs through my fingers, and I feel the moistness of your body. I am grounded, held close in your embrace. The grass nestles me in softness and I am strengthened by the simplicity of your care. I am healed by your love, Mother.

Seeking to pull the warmth of your golden rays to me, I reach for you in the sky and feel your heat like that of a lover, quickening my pulse, my Yoni longing for surrender.

Earth and Water, Air and Fire, you surround me all my days. All that my eyes gaze upon is of you, within me and without. Creatrix, Mother of All Life, I thank you for this experience of... being in your Embrace.

The Elements

If you were a chemistry student, you would be familiar with the Periodic Table of Elements. The following definition applies to elements found in all matter, which are listed in the periodic table:

Element – Chemical elements are the fundamental materials of which all matter is composed. From the modern viewpoint a substance that cannot be broken down or reduced further is, by definition an element.

Elements in the Spiritual World - The four elements of the spiritual world are present as four typical manifestations of "energy" that show up as distinct kinds of experiences on the physical plane and four qualities of psycho-spiritual abilities. These four elements go by the names Fire, Earth, Air and Water. In the spiritual realm these four substances are seen as necessary to the creation and sustenance of life. Each element is associated with one of the four directions, a particular tool, certain qualities and powers (which exist in both the physical world and within each person), and certain colors, life forms and natural phenomena.

I like to call these elements the Elder Children of the Mother. They were First Born before all else and as such, are the building blocks from which all else is made. They are the primary spiritual helpers that we call upon in our magical work. We can call on them from outside ourselves or we can call on them from within, for they are everywhere, inside and out. We attribute them to certain directions, but that is really for our own convenience. Where they are placed varies with each spiritual tradition.

They have many correspondences such as goddesses, energies, seasons, animals, plants, birds, psychological characteristics, activities, stones, colors, etc.

When we cast a circle, it is a natural part of the casting to invite the Elements into our sacred space, along with the particular attributes they bring that are needed for our desired task.

Because they carry such importance in our spiritual work, considerable time is spent learning about them so that the "feel" of them becomes a natural part of you. For truly when you bring them into your sacred space, it is from within that they come.

A good way to learn about them is to spend one quarter of the year on each Element. So, in setting out your year, be sure to include a focus on the Elements. This is easily accomplished by assigning one Element per Season of the Year.

Season	Element	Begins
Spring	Air	Imbolc – February 1
Summer	Fire	Beltane – May 1
Fall	Water	Lammas – August 1
Winter	Earth	Samhain – October 31

As you travel through the season pay attention to everything around you. Jot down all those things you can identify as the Element you are working with. Keep notes in your journal. Include things you see, touch, feel, hear, and taste.

What follows are some traditional associations for each of the four Elements.

Some Attributes of the Elements

The Element is Air and it is placed in the East.

The Attributes of Air are:
> Free mind, joy, creativity, imagination, clearing, illumination, divination, mental stimulation, philosophy, mindfulness, awareness, perception, and clearing.
> The Energy of Air is swift, mercurial, and changeable.
> The Traditional Colors of Air are White, Yellow, Scarlet, Peach, Turquoise, Blue, and Gold.

Some Sacred Spirits of Air are
> Danu - Goddess of creativity
> Athena - Goddess of wisdom
> Kwan Yin - Goddess of mindfulness
> Nuit - Goddess of the skies
> Sylphs - elemental spirits of Air

Some Animals associated with Air are:
> Doves - for messages of peace and illumination
> Hawk - for focus and perception
> Eagle - for philosophy and ideals
> Wolf - for communication and perception
> Deer - for perception, awareness
> Raccoon - for thinking
> Cardinals - for creativity

Some Minerals associated with Air are:
> White or clear fluorite - for illumination and creativity
> Moonstone - for receptivity to illumination
> Turquoise - for focus and awareness
> Single-point crystals - for perception
> Amethyst - for meditation and illumination
> Rhodochrosite - for brain stimulation
> Azurite - for brain clarity
> Citrine - for clarity and purification

Some Plant Helpers associated with Air are:
> Wildflowers - for creativity
> Spearmint, Lavender, Clover, and Sage - for meditation incenses

Some Air activities include divination, friendly debates, the martial arts, meditation, flower arranging, Tai Chi, and vision quests.

The Element is Fire and it is placed in the South.

The Attributes of Fire are faith and trust, transformation, change, elusiveness, innocence, vulnerability, strength, protection, and passion. Relationships with others, with self, and with nature.

The Energy of Fire is quick and rapid.

The Traditional Colors of Fire are Red, Orange, Scarlet, Yellow, White, and the Blue of flame.

Some Sacred Spirits of Fire are:

Bridget - Goddess of the inner flame of life and creation
Pele - Goddess of purification and upheaval
Hestia - Goddess of strength in women
Sekhmet – Egyptian Goddess
Salamanders - Elemental spirits of Fire

Some Animals of Fire are:
Porcupine - for protection and to prick you into action
Badger - for protection in conflict
Coyote - for protection in tricky situations
Fox - for elusiveness and innocence
Hawk - for protection and relationships
Mouse - for vulnerability and elusiveness
Cats - of all sorts

Some Minerals of Fire are:
Pink Carnelian - for kinships and relationships
Red Carnelian - for strength and protection, faith
Gold Amber - for clarity in relationships
Red Amber - for courage, faith
Amber Calcite - for relationships, trust
Blue Amber - for shamanic journeys of purification, inner flame
Yellow and Gold Fluorite - for personal protection on journeys
Fire Opal - for deep inner vision, physical purification and cleansing
Steel - for strength in trials of life
Iron Ore - for courage, protection
Lava - for purification and upheaval

Some Plant Helpers of Fire are:
   Purification Incenses, protection incenses, sage, sweetgrass, juniper, myrrh, thyme, frankincense, close, cinnamon, cedar, and dragon's blood.

The Element is Water and it is placed in the West.

The attributes of Water are inner knowing, dreams, emotions, feelings, introspection, shamanic journeys, and healing, balancing active and receptive energies.

The Energy of Water is tidal - it ebbs and flows.
The Traditional Colors of Water are Blue-green, Aqua, Blue-grey, Black, Indigo, and the White of sea foam in moonlight.

Some Sacred Spirits of Water are:
   Isis - Goddess of the rivers of life
   Arianrhod - Celtic Goddess of the Moon and Earth
   Hecate - Goddess of the Dark Moon
   Yemaya – African Goddess of the Sea
   Undines - elemental spirits of water

Some Animals of Water are:
   Sea Mammals - for psychic communication
   Sea Birds - for uplifted emotions
   Heron - for intuition and organization
   Jaguar - for shamanic journeys
   Raven - for dreams and inner knowing
   Bear - for introspection and especially for healing

Elk- for feelings and emotions
Fish - of all types, for swimming in the tides of emotions

Some Minerals of Water are:
Aquamarine - for inner journeys, serenity
Blue-colored crystals - for psychic flow
River Rocks - for emotions
Ocean Rocks - for healing and emotion
Silver - for intuition
Amethyst - for inner journeys, soothing emotions
Mercury - for changeable emotions
White Coral - for flexibility
Rainbow Crystals - for shamanic journeys
Blue Fluorite - for shamanic journeys and dreams
Double-Terminated Crystals - for healing energies

Some Plant Helpers of Water:
Journey incenses, dream teas, lotus, chamomile, sandalwood, jasmine, mugwort, raspberry, camphor, catnip, vanilla, cherry, violet, and hibiscus.

The Element is Earth and it is placed in the North.

The Attributes of Earth are wisdom, abundance, practicality, symbols, ritual, ceremony, prosperity, wisdom, teaching and learning, and patience

The Energy or pace of Earth is steady, rhythmic; it is the Heartbeat of Mother Earth.

The Traditional Colors of Earth are Green, Violet, Brown, Black, White, and the Deep Blue of the Earth as seen from space

Some Sacred Spirits of Earth are:
- Gaia - Earth Mother Goddess
- Demeter - Goddess of grain and abundance
- Rhea – Goddess - mother of all deities
- Gnomes - elemental spirits of Earth

Some Animals of Earth are:
- Buffalo - for wisdom and practicality
- Wolf - for teaching earth wisdom
- Owl - for sacred knowledge
- Dragon - for symbols
- Stag Deer - for ritual and ceremony
- Heron - from organized wisdom from intuition
- Mythical Beasts - of all types, for learning the symbols of   wisdom

Some Minerals of Earth are:
- Crystal formations or clusters - for gathering wisdom and energy
- Dark Crystals - for sacred knowledge and ceremony
- Onyx - for practicality
- Jasper - for earth wisdom
- Aventurine - for prosperity
- Green Jade - for growth and prosperity
- Black Jade - for patience

Deep Violet Fluorite - for ritual and symbols
Royal Azurite - for symbols and DNA codes
Marble - for steadfast practicality
Amethyst - for ritual, wisdom and ceremony

Some Plant Helpers of Earth are:
Oak Trees - for all magic, ritual, ceremony
Redwood Trees - for sacred wisdom
Myrrh, Sagebrush, Patchouli, Magnolia- for ceremonial incenses.

Questions to ask yourself and suggestions for things to do:

Begin your own study of the Elements. Choose the Element of the season you are in and begin noticing things around you and naming all of those things of that Element. Write them down. This will include things you see, eat, taste, feel and think. Words, associations, anything you like. There is no right or wrong. This is your identification. Include this "naming" in your journal. Continue with the same Element until the next seasonal change.

Creating Sacred Space

For the purpose of our work, we will define sacred space as a place set apart to use for sacred work. Meditation, prayer, ritual, magical work, any type of activity whose purpose is to achieve a transcended state is better accomplished if performed in the right space both externally and internally. Actually, I believe that all space is sacred including our own "internal" space. So the purpose of what we do in creating sacred space is to facilitate the recognition of it being sacred! It is like any magical act—the process is changing our own perception, changing our reality of "what is!" The process can be done entirely in the mind, but is better when done with others, by using symbols as part of the process.

If you are lucky you will have available for your work a separate room, one that can be set up and used only by you, not to be entered except for the purpose designed. If this is not possible then the next option is to select a corner of a room that can be made private and is perhaps, little used by others. Most people use their bedroom as it has less traffic by outsiders and can be kept private. If this is not possible then select any area that can easily be made "special" but can also be easily disguised and kept private from others. Any objects you place in this space should easily blend into other decoration and not be noticeable to others. The last option is to set up and create your space each time you have the need. Any items used could be stored in a special box or basket and taken out when needed. An outside area is also wonderful in good weather.

The first thing you need to do is select the place you are going to set up your sacred space. Physically clean it. This means that you sweep, vacuum, dust, and put away all clutter or any other reminders of disorganization in your life.

It is very important at this point to know what you are going to use this space for. It can be used for many purposes or any one single purpose such as: meditation, affirmation work, worship, divination or any other personal work you wish to do. Having made this decision you next decide what you want in this space and collect it. Things to consider are those things that will trigger your senses to heighten your awareness while using the space. Here is a list of suggestions:

SENSE	ITEMS
Sight	- Objects to look at, figurines, candles, and flowers, items to represent deity, items to represent the elements.
Hearing	- CD/tape player, CD's/tapes, musical instruments, drums, rattles, bells, etc.
Touch	- Personal, memorable items that you may wish to hold.
Smell	- Incense, potpourri, oil burner and oils.
Taste	- Food or drink and containers for them.

Now it is time to arrange what you have collected. Place each object at the place it can be most easily used. Keep in mind your area's purpose.

Now that you have your area ready to use, it is time to prepare yourself for the spiritual work ahead. The actual spiritual cleansing and use of the sacred space should be done when you are sure of no interruptions. Prepare your body by keeping to a light fast for at least six hours. I prefer what is called a non-killing fast in which nothing is consumed that has lost its life for your consumption. This would include not eating any animal products, root vegetables, etc. Mentally prepare by planning and thinking about the work you will be doing.

When you are ready to begin, take the phone off the hook or turn off the ringer. If you like, take a bath using salt or special herbs in your bath water. Use visualization techniques to see any negativity being removed from your body and going down the drain as the bath water drains away. I like to have music and candle light while doing this. When finished, enter your space, wearing nothing or a special garment for this purpose only.

Always try to begin your work with a deep centering and grounding. This can be done with your breath; follow it in and follow it out by taking long slow breaths. Find your own personal center and focus your attention there until you feel calm. You may even visualize yourself as a tree sending roots down into the earth while reaching upward into the sky with your branches.

Next you need to clear the area of any negativity. You may use clearing incense, such as frankincense, sage, sandalwood, etc. Either mentally or verbally, bless and consecrate the area with the elements of air, fire, water and earth. This can be done using salt water (earth & water) and burning incense (fire & air). See the circle building around you. You may fill your space with white light, or any other color you choose. See it above, around and below you. Invite the spirits of the elements and your deities to join you in your work. If you would prefer, you may also bless and consecrate with other things more meaningful to you at the time. You may just wish to use your concept of the divine and that's all.
When all this is done it is time to do the work you set out to do. This may be some magical work, meditation, divination, etc. When your work is complete thank all you have invited in and open your space.

As you continue to use your sacred space you will learn many new things. Explore the use of music in your work. Explore how color affects you. Try choosing different rocks to have around. Remember to play, have fun and grow with each new experience!

I would like to interject, at this point, that none of this is necessary! All of the steps, procedures, and symbols are for you—triggers to your inner mind and body. The more rituals you do, and the more often you create sacred space, the more you will realize that the process happens inside of your own body and the "stuff" is not always necessary to use. You can be as elaborate or as simple as your own personal needs dictate.

Whatever you do, please don't be afraid you are doing something "wrong". Everyone has a different method and no one method is any more "correct" than any other. What "works" for you is "right" for you. Be open to experimentation and enjoy whatever you have created!

Now that you have the basics of creating sacred space, we can learn about casting a Circle for the purpose of doing ritual and magical work. The point of casting a circle is to create a container for your work. In your work you will be building and moving energy, and it is important to contain it until it is time to release it.

There are as many ways to cast a Circle as your imagination can allow!!! It can be so simple as to be all in your mind, or as elaborate as you desire. There is no right or wrong way, simply your way.

What helps me decide how I want to cast my circle is to remember why I want to do this particular ritual and magical work. What is the purpose for doing this? Once I know my purpose, then I can think about various ways to create my space.

I have never needed to spend a lot of time trying to keep things out of my Circle, as I don't invite anything in that is not for my highest good. I feel that only that which I invite will attend! What I do try is to build a positive container for the ritual work. Then, I take a look at that work and decide what ingredients I need to make the magic happen!

I might wish to create a visible boundary, one that I can see as I move about my space. I can draw it on the floor if the flooring allows for that. I can mark my space with rocks that I have collected. I can lay down tape; I can sprinkle flower petals around the boundary; I can send magical blue energy out from my fingers or blade to create the same effect. Whatever I use, I also use my own energy to mentally create edges and boundaries for my work. I enclose myself within a circle, from every direction, horizontally, vertically, ending up with something much like a bubble.

When I do my Moons honoring the trees, I use the rocks I have collected over the years, thirteen of them, to mark my sacred space.

I begin by sweeping and cleaning where I am to work. Then I lay my stones, one by one around the circle, marking the space where I will work between the worlds.

I create an altar for myself, anywhere in the space works, in the center, or in one of the four directions (East, South, West, or North). My favorite location is the North, for that is where I consider the home of the Gods and the source of Great Wisdom. North is where I come "home."

On my altar I like to have a representation of each of the four Elements. They can be very simple: salt for Earth, a shell for Water (or my chalice), a feather for Air, and a candle for Fire. I also have a Goddess candle and something to represent Goddess. I also work with two blades*, so those are there as well. If I am going to need other visible symbols I will place those on my altar as well, unless the ritual calls for them to be placed elsewhere. Sometimes I create altars in all of the four directions, giving each Element an altar of its own. On those I might place various symbols representing them.

I use a compass to determine my directions before beginning. If I don't have one, I try to determine those points using signs in nature.

As I said earlier, I begin my casting by walking to the North, mentally acknowledging my "home" there. I then take a minute to ground and center.

I walk to the East drawing my Circle, seeing the Circle as I create it. Then, facing the East, I evoke Air. Using whatever words I feel appropriate, feeling Air, sensing Air, becoming Air, I call Air from within me to be fully present in my sacred space. I mark the point in the East by drawing a pentagram to seal that quadrant.

I continue to draw my circle. I walk to the South and stand facing in that direction to evoke Fire. Using whatever words I feel appropriate, feeling Fire, sensing Fire, becoming Fire, I call Fire from within me to be fully present in my sacred space. I mark the point in the South by drawing a pentagram to seal that quadrant.

Again walking and drawing my circle, I walk to the West and turn, facing the West. I evoke Water. Using whatever words I feel appropriate, feeling Water, sensing Water, becoming Water, I call Water from within me to be fully present in my sacred space. I mark the point in the West by drawing a pentagram to seal that quadrant.

I continue walking to the North to complete the circle and stand facing the North. I evoke Earth. Using whatever words I feel appropriate, feeling Earth, sensing Earth, becoming Earth, I call Earth from within me to be fully present in my sacred space. I mark the point in the North by drawing a pentagram to seal that quadrant. That completes marking the edges of my sacred space.

I turn and walk to the Center of my Circle. The Center of my Circle is where I fully connect with all that is. Having brought the powers of the Four Elements into my space, I now look to the sky and see a portal opening to other realms and then look down at the Earth, seeing an axis connecting what is above to that which is below. Standing very still at the center of my Circle, I go within, seeking all that is sacred and holy of myself, finding the love and compassion of my heart, expanding my own sense of Goddess, She Who is Divine. Reaching my consciousness out into the Universe I pull She Who is All into my sacred space, merging and becoming one with me. I offer thanksgiving and blessing for Her Divine Presence. There are times I may wish to call a particular Goddess, selecting Her based on the work being done.

At this point in time, my Circle is created and I declare it so. I may also choose to build more energy within my Circle even though I already built energy as I created it. I might now infuse the whole area with certain colors, or by using my heart chakra, fill it with love. If others are present, we may sing, chant, dance, or find another way to increase and build the energy around us.

It is at this point that the actual work is done. I may make a declaration of what my work is. If it is a special occasion that I am marking, and others are present, I may offer an explanation or a telling of why we are honoring this event. My statement will be clear as to the work we are doing. When the work is done, we may make something in our sacred space. We may release those things no longer needed. We may share stories, make statements of intent, do a healing, mark a special passage for someone, meditate, or take a journey. If we are healing or manifesting we may again raise even more energy, called building a cone of power. Once the cone reaches its peak we'll release it to go where it is intended.

Once the work has been finished, it is a tradition at this point to share a chalice with the Goddess and those present. Some also include cakes or food of some kind as a special feast. In passing the Chalice we honor the Goddess and each other with special blessings. I then close my Circle by reversing everything I have done, releasing all that I have invited to my space.

This was a very simple Circle Casting. They can also be even simpler and entirely within your mind without ever lifting a finger. I do believe however, that going through the motions is critical, especially in the beginning of your practice.

I encourage you to experiment. You will find all kinds of information on how to do a casting, but some places will tell you their way is the "correct" way. Please keep in mind that there are as many ways to do this as there are women casting Circles. Each way is unique and perfect. Know what you want within your sacred space and then create it! Play, and allow your inner child to explore. Find new ways to mark your Circle's edge. Investigate methods of clearing negativity and sacred ways to honor the divine. Search your heart. You have all the answers.

Questions to ask yourself and suggestions for things to do:

Have you created a space in your home that is sacred for you?

If not, take the time now to create one for yourself, a place of calm, one that suggests what's sacred to you. What would you have there?

What about outside? Have you a sacred altar in your garden? Have you ever taken a walk and created spontaneously, a small shrine in nature, something up beside a tree perhaps? If you haven't, make plans one day to go walk and be observant of small places that call to you, as well as little objects that seem the perfect thing to place on an altar for Goddess. Small rocks and feathers are among those things you may want to collect, and once you have found what feels like the right place, build an altar. Simple is *key*. Blend your altar with what is around it, and if anyone were to see it, they would know that someone had a sacred moment, and made an offering of love.

In what ways could you invite the Elements into your Circle?

How would you invite Goddess?

The next time you wish to light a candle for someone, first cast a circle. Think of what you want to have within your Circle, what attributes of each Element you want present, and if you want a specific Goddess to aid you in your work. How would you invite Her? What would you have in your Circle that might honor Her?

Take time over the next month or so to practice casting your Circles. Try different ways. Create poetry for your invocations. Sing the elements in. Dance with Goddess. Allow your inner child to explore and play.

The Importance of Ritual

The reason and the importance of ritual in all world religions and spiritual paths, is the achievement of a more awakened consciousness, to touch on all of the physical senses in such a way as to awaken one to a higher level of spiritual awareness. Think, for example, of the movements of the ministers on TV. Everything moves in a certain order, and if this order is not followed, people are unsettled.

It also helps to do things in a certain order, over and over, so that they become automatic, and the procedure does not interfere with the ideals in mind. For instance, when doing a healing within the circle, we can concentrate on the healing and not look at each other wondering what we are going to do next.

The order of the ritual is simple, the circle is cast, censed and sprinkled, the quarters are called, the Goddess is invited to attend and then the work begins. Once you have the words you want to say down, you can concentrate more on drawing energy to work with. Air gives you soft energy, Fire gives hot, Water gives cold and soft energy, and Earth gives you cool and hard energy. Each Element adds to the mix to create the necessary power. The calling of the Goddess then adds a broad range of energy, which binds the other four together.

Whether you are working alone or in a group, after a short time, the basics of how you work will become automatic. The thing you need to watch though, after you become totally comfortable with your routine, is that the movements don't lose their importance. If you let them become just a series of steps, not a whole entity, they will lose their effectiveness. A way to help prevent that is to add creativity to the mix. Find new and appropriate ways each time, matching intent with methods. I have been to circles where everyone seems to just be going through the motions. They raise no energy, and you leave the ritual feeling kind of let down. Please know that this can happen to anyone, even an experienced ritualist, but it generally happens in a circle where not only the priestess, but also the people within that circle have little or no training in working with energy. The power of ritual comes from a fully open participant, all senses activated and emotions raised to direct energy. Remember, without energy, you have no magic. Magic is like a light bulb; it only works if you add enough energy. Do not confuse the exhaustion that comes after working difficult magic with the dull, flat feeling of energy-free magic. One is distinctly the "is that all there is?" feeling, while the other is the elated exhaustion that comes after a finished race, or a wonderful rush horizontally.

When first coming to this path your work is mostly solitary. Even later on there will be times that you may not be able to attend circle with others. This can happen due to time constraints and other problems that make solitary work a necessity and group work a luxury. If you are going to find time to celebrate the holidays and full moons at all, it is better to do so alone than not at all.

It is also best to establish a ritual that is comfortable for you which does not wear you out. If solitary or practicing with a sole partner, this is not difficult, it just takes some thought and planning.

Ritual can also be easier if you have props—symbols as visual reminders of your intended work. However, none are really needed. If you choose to use symbols, you may wish to use quarter candles, an athame, a dish of salt, bowl or glass of water, some incense, and an altar candle. A glass of wine, fruit juice, or water and something like cookies, crackers, or bread is nice for grounding at the closing of your Circle. And finally, symbols of the actual magic at hand!

If you are meeting for a group ritual, offer to assist the person hosting the ritual. Even if they refuse, always offer your services. Probably the hardest role in the circle is that of the priestess or the facilitator of the Circle. On her shoulders rests the responsibility of making sure all the necessary equipment is assembled, that everyone knows their part, that all materials are ready, and that the goal (the work to be done) is not only understood, but is agreed upon by the entire group. They must also make sure everyone is playing well with others, which in itself can be a challenge. All of this has to be done before the priestess can have everyone standing ready for a circle.

Then she is responsible for casting the circle, calling the Goddess, directing everyone in raising energy, noting any weak spots in the circle and filling them with her own energy, deciding when the energy is strong enough, doing the actual work, then directing the dismissal of the elementals and the deities.

She must also be cordial and directive until everyone goes home. It can be quite exhausting.

The beauty of a Goddess Circle is that, as a general rule, most of the women (if they have had any instruction at all) understand that everyone shares in maintaining the energy and doing the work.

Sometimes, in spite of the best-laid plans, you will over-extend yourself. It just happens, it's part of life. The trick is not to let your magical pursuits leave you unable to take care of everything else.

Remember, in your own space, you are your own priestess. Working alone, you may not be able to raise the same amount of energy as a large group at first. Yet, on the other hand, you don't have to raise enough power to make up for less adept members. In any group you will have stronger, more experienced people than yourself, as well as those who are not as strong.

In the creation of magic, you must think, act, and be responsible. Magic requires thought and carries full accountability. You must decide on what is within your realm both ethically and realistically. If you do not agree on a goal that your group wants to work toward, say so. They deserve to know of your lack of conviction on any point, and it would probably be better if you did not participate in something you do not agree with. You will only drain the power from their work with your negativity. Likewise, if someone does not want to help you with a spell that you feel is necessary, don't grovel and beg, be polite and thank them for their honesty. Their lack of conviction could seriously undermine your work; don't berate them for their show of integrity.

If you do not agree on all points, but would still like to help your friends, offer to do that by lighting a candle, or sending them positive energy. You would then ask for blessings for them personally, not for blessings towards their intended goal. That way you have helped and have also kept your integrity intact. This eases the laws of cause and effect.

My goal for each of you, whether you choose to follow a path similar to mine or not, is to open your mind and heart to help yourself always be your authentic self. Whether or not your goals and ethics match mine, and if you branch off in your own direction, it is entirely acceptable to use your conscience as your guide. If you finish this book knowing what you believe, with the convictions to act on those beliefs, I will have accomplished what I have set out to do in writing this book.

Questions to ask yourself and things to do:

Write down the many ways in which you have already used ritual in your life.

Begin your practice of writing your own rituals. Begin with very simple ideas. Perhaps you can try your hand at the next Sabbat—a seasonal ritual to honor the coming of that season.

Create small daily ritual practices to bring about a mind-state of honoring and gratitude into your daily reality.

Energy Work

In other chapters, I have made reference to the term energy. I have made comments about raising energy and sensing energy. This chapter is devoted to the topic of energy, basically what it is and what you can do to become more aware of it. We will discuss ground, centering, seeing, and feeling energy. This chapter is by no means a complete treatise on energy, but it does offer you some basic exploration. I do not profess to give you all the answers; instead, I invite you to explore on your own how to become fully attuned to your energy and the energies of those around you.

Centering ~ Be a Tree

Make your body comfortable, taking easy slow breaths, in and out. As you do that, imagine the breath coming in to be pure and clean, refreshing. Take it into your body feeling it nourishing and replenishing you. Do this for a minute or two.

Locate within yourself what you perceive as your personal center. For most people this is in the lower abdomen, slightly below the naval. Focus your attention to the spot that is your center.

If you are standing, align your upper body over your center and your lower body beneath it. Place your feet apart, in line with your shoulders, and slightly bend your knees and heals on the ground.

If you are sitting, align your upper body over your center, sitting straight-up but not rigid. Your legs may be crossed Indian style or straight out in front of you.

Once you locate and focus on your center, imagine a long root growing out of that spot descending down into the ground (floor). Send it deeply into the Earth. As it descends watch it branch out into many shoots extending all around you. If this feels awkward to you, you may also send the roots down through your feet.

Feel those roots move and grow, attaching and intertwining, holding fast and drawing Her cool moist energy up into your body. Be still with this for a minute or two.

Once that is done, feel the upper part of your body becoming the branches, your arms reaching out for the Sun. Your branches will reach high into the sky as well as reaching wide all around you. Allow your branches to absorb the energy of the sun and sky. It is warm and vitalizing.

Now feel these two energies coming together, the cool moist energy of the Earth and the warm vitalizing energy of the Sun. Take those energies and bring them together inside you and swirl them around, mixing and blending them both with your own energies. Allow yourself to breathe easily, releasing all the cares of the day. Be at peace. Be alive. Be centered.

Grounding

Grounding is establishing a connection between our energy and the world around us; it lets us keep our psychic balance. This is not the same as charging or discharging, as there may not be a change in the level of energy; it is merely our energy merging with the energy around us. We ground primarily through our feet, hands, and eyes. So, when we want to ground we can walk or stomp into the ground, touch a tree or a wall, and look around to root us in our bodies and in the present. This is an important process because charging with energy will cause increased feeling in our bodies, and intensify our emotions and thoughts. When this happens and we are not grounded it can be frightening and we may feel out of touch with our bodies. The antidote is grounding. As we experiment with charging and discharging, you will also need to work with grounding. For now, remember to feel your feet and hands, and to look around you.

If after a ritual or a meditation, you feel spaced out, it is important to reconnect. This is easily accomplished by doing any of the following things:

> Make eye contact with another
> Hug someone
> Eat something
> Drink something
> Touch someone

Touch something
Touch the Earth
Hug a tree

Personal Energy

Personal energy is called by a variety of names, depending on the cultural influences of the speaker. It is called prana, chi, ki, life force, etc. We can enhance our own personal energy by many different techniques. The easiest one is by using breath. There are many systems that teach breathing techniques—all sorts of patterns and rhythms to apply to breathing. But for us, right now, simply the act of taking time to do a few deep-cleansing breaths will be sufficient. Be comfortable. Inhale slowly and deeply, using the muscles of the abdomen to draw in the air. Feel the air enter and fill your lungs. Hold that air for a couple of seconds and gently release, allowing all of the air to leave. Pause a couple of seconds and then begin the in-breathing again. Do this for a minute or two and feel your energy becoming vitalized.

For sending energy, you will need to find someone to work with you. Sit facing your partner. Place the index finger of your right hand on the index finger of the other person's left hand. Find your center. Breathe into your center. As you breathe into your center imagine the air coming in to energize your center. If you can, see the energy inside you expand. If you cannot see it, don't worry. Just imagine that you do. When it feels right, mentally send that energy to your finger tip, and touch the other person's finger tip. Send the energy to them. Practice this for a few minutes, and then reverse this so the other person can try it.

Now, do the same exercises with four of your finger tips touching four of theirs. After both of you have tried this, do it again touching the whole palm of your hand to theirs. Make sure to notice any minor differences each time you try this.

Now, sitting while facing each other, rub your palms against those of your partner. Feel the heat being generated in the palms of your own hands as you do. Then slightly pull apart your palms to feel the energy linked between your own two hands. Slowly move your hands out, gently observing and feeling the energy between them until you sense you are at the edge. Do this until you reach the end of the part of energy you can feel. Then, gently push back against the energy. It should feel like you have a sort of spongy ball between the palms of your hands. If it doesn't work the first time, please don't be discouraged. It often takes several tries. Just start over and do it again.

Now rub your hands together and place your palms up against your partner's palms. Hold the palms together evenly with all fingers touching. Experience what you feel. Warmth, tingling? Begin deep breathing. Slowly begin moving your palms away from each other. Experience the energy flow. What do you feel? Keep going. What do you feel now?

Continue moving the palms apart until you no longer experience an energy flow. It may not be far at first, but will get farther with practice. Now move the palms back in slightly, as you continue your meditative breathing. What do you feel? Keep moving inward, what are you feeling now? Experiment while slowly moving in and out. What does *this* feel like? Practice this exercise daily.

You can send energy through other parts of your body as well. Try doing this each day. Try sending energy through your eyes, through your chakras, even your feet! Also consider the energy of surroundings and other life forms. Experiment also with stones, herbs, and colors, etc. Try to "feel" others.

Observe your personal energy patterns and flows. When do you have energy ups? Downs? What days do you feel up? Down? Find your body's flow pattern. Keep a record. Notice the moon's cycle, waxing, full, waning and planetary positions. Keep a log of this information.

Psychic Self-defense

The best protection you have is your belief that you are totally protected, that you are impervious to psychic attack.

We are innately protected in believing that nothing is stronger than we are. Equal, perhaps, but not stronger. The only way anything can get to us is if we allow it to. If we refuse to allow entry of negative psychic energy it cannot enter! Practice psychic self-defense with these techniques:

- Energy flow reversal with eyes - Energy typically moves out of your right eye and in with your left. Practice and see if you can feel the in-and-out flow. Work with a partner. Once you can feel the flow, try to reverse it. Describe your sensations.
- Learn about building shields - Reasons for forming a shield include emotional enhancement and personal protection.
- Research other methods of protection using stones, herbs, incense, salt & herb baths, candles, and tone.

Life is energy, an energy that is continually charging and discharging as it moves through our bodies. Energy moves in and out as we breathe, growing stronger when we breathe deeply, and weaker when we breathe shallowly. As we collect a large charge of energy we feel the need to discharge. This can happen in many ways, laughter or tears, singing or screaming, and especially lovemaking. These are all ways people discharge energy. All life forms engage in this process, even the Earth Herself is alive. The wind moves the Earth's energy, building it across distances until it discharges as a storm, which waters the forest below, which in turn exchanges energy with the animals that live within them.

We can feel our own aura and gain a sense of our individual energy by rubbing our hands together quickly, holding our palms together, and then slowly separating our hands until we feel a sense of being at a boundary. For most people, this will be at about three inches. As we continue to feel the energy, it will expand, especially if we are breathing fully. As we press in, we feel a slight resistance, and as we pull our hands apart they will feel as if they are covered with something soft. When doing this exercise we are consciously beginning to build a charge, and so when we finish it is also good to release that energy by grounding ourselves.

By definition, energy is a life force. Everything is energy. We, ourselves, are energy bodies. The only thing that keeps us from using the energy that we are is ourselves. One of the most critical things to learn in your work as a witch is how to sense, feel, and utilize the energy of your own body and the energy available in abundance in our Universe. Each of us has our own particular set of sensing skills that seem to work better for us than the others. Typically, we have one dominant sensing skill and another that is slightly less active. But in fact, all of our senses are present and can be opened for our use with practice. I believe they are just underused and therefore somewhat dormant.

The two primary ways of sensing energy are visual and kinesthetic. Of course, we can smell, taste, and hear energy. And, if we are truly in tune, we "know" the energy. However, we don't often think of sensing energy in those ways. Those senses are mostly utilized in other ways equally vital to our connection with the web of life, and they need to be developed and fine-tuned if we are to work in harmony with nature.

For now, let us work with the visual and kinesthetic senses as they apply to working with energy.

The energy that moves through us animates our aura, a field caused by the interaction between the energy pulsating within our physical bodies, cycles of emotions, patterns of thought, and our spirit. As the energy pulsates, the different levels of our being vibrate to produce a perceptible field that surrounds us like a translucent, multi-colored bubble.

Auras can be seen, often with the inner eye rather than our physical ones, and they may also be felt. All of us feel auras without even realizing it. For example, while standing in line at the grocery store to check out, someone comes up behind me. I may feel a sense of discomfort if that person behind me gets too close, feeling the need to move forward a bit. In another scenario you might be having a conversation with someone, and as they speak to you they might get excited and move nearer to you, at a distance that instinctively feels uncomfortable. They feel like they are "in your face" and you move backwards without really thinking about it, seeking a more comfortable distance.

In both of these cases, the other person entered our aura to a point that was uncomfortable for us. Our senses picked up on this instinctively and sent a message to our brains to adjust our positions.

We can train ourselves to both see and feel auras. Some will be more successful visually; others will have greater success in the sense of touch. As I move my hands over a person's body, perhaps 4 to 5 inches out from the surface, I feel a slight push when I am at the edge. For me in my healing work, I find "areas of distress" by the temperature changes felt in my palms. Sometimes the area feels warmer and sometimes colder. Both are, however, signals for me to investigate.

When I do chakra work on someone, my sense of touch registers where the chakras are, and how they feel to my hands (warm, cold, and the direction the energy is moving). By feeling the energy in the chakras, I can do my healing work to balance them.

Others see these things, sometimes in colors, sometimes in just darker or lighter shades. I do not *see* so it would be hard for me to explain what another might perceive. However, we quickly learn once we begin to practice our skills, exactly how we sense energy.

Now, see if you can find a partner to play with using energy. Decide who goes first. This participant should slowly approach the other with hands out-stretched until an aura is felt. It should feel like a barrier. You might experience a slight push to your hands. Slowly feel around the body at that place, searching for different sensations. You might feel hot spots, cold spots, push or pull, or tingling. It will vary with each individual. Talk out loud about what you feel to your partner. The person being "felt" should respond with any information that might help. When done, reverse roles.

Sometime when you can either sit or stand, try observing another individual—can you see any kind of color around the edges of their body? It helps to look with what we call soft-focused eyes, as well as having a clean background behind the person being observed. Do this whenever you get the chance and you will be surprised one day!

Here are some terms to help you with the language of energy:

Charging

Charging is increasing the energy in our whole-self which comes from breathing, the drawing in of the life force. When we charge up we increase our awareness of our bodies, emotions, thoughts and spirit. Charging will feel good to us to the extent that we feel comfortable with our lives, at peace with ourselves, and it will feel natural and pleasurable.

Discharging

Discharging is decreasing the energy in our whole-self that comes from the expression of our charged awareness of our bodies, emotions, thoughts and spirit. We discharge in many different ways that are suited to the type of awareness we have. Physically we may feel good in our bodies, or jittery and unable to relax. Emotionally we may laugh or cry, feel love or fear, trust or anger. Intellectually, we may have a "brainstorm" or obsess about details. And spiritually, we may either feel the "wonder of life" or that life is pointless.

Energy Economy

The balance we keep between energy charges and discharges.

Streaming

Streaming is a pleasurable feeling of energy circulating vertically, up and down in our bodies.

Expansion

Expansion is an increase in the size of our aura with an accompanying decrease in its density so that the total amount of energetic charge remains constant.

Contraction

Contraction is a decrease in the size of our aura with an accompanying increase in its density so that the total amount of energetic charge remains constant.

Pulsation

Pulsation is the regular cycle of expansion and contraction caused by natural cycles such as breathing, the heartbeat, or waking and sleeping. Breathing is especially important because it is one cycle that, though normally unconscious, we can consciously change at will.

Counter-Pulsation

Counter-pulsation is anything that opposes the process of pulsation. It can be caused by either the conflict of two pulsations that are not synchronized or it can be a more general deadening of the natural energetic streaming.

Grounding

Grounding is feeling an energetic connection to the people and the world around us. We ground through our feet, hands and eyes.

Muscular Armoring

Muscular armoring is the tensing of muscles against the natural pulsation of energy. We do this either to shield ourselves from being hurt by other people in situations outside our control, or to block experiencing parts of ourselves that we feel are dangerous. When life becomes too intense we tighten our muscles or change our breathing to numb our feelings, the same way we did when we were infants, unable to clearly speak our needs. Although muscular armoring can gain us enough strength to stand intense feelings, if we continually deny ourselves the opportunity to discharge those feelings they will solidify and stay with our physical bodies long after the initial storm has passed.

Boundaries

Boundaries are the limits we set between ourselves and the world. When our boundaries are normal, we can open them to allow interaction or close them to restrict it as we choose—this is how we deal with the people around us. Setting boundaries lets us define who we are by differentiating us from others, and is a normal and necessary step in growing up. However, when our boundaries are violated, we may have problems setting limits in a normal manner. If our boundaries are too hard, we isolate ourselves from others, thereby cutting off outside sources of nourishment. If our personal boundaries are too soft, we cannot separate ourselves from others—leaving us too open and vulnerable to exploitation. There are other types of boundaries I would also like to mention:

- Physical Boundary - Our physical boundary is the first boundary we set as an infant. We learn where our bodies begin and end as we explore the world by touch. As this border becomes instinctive, it lets us know who we allow to touch us and who we will not, when we want to be held and when we want to be left alone. As adults the physical boundary lets us know who we will permit physical intimacy with and who we will not.

- Emotional Boundary - An emotional boundary is the second to be set and allows us to choose who is emotionally close to us. We learn to set it by feeling comfortable with our own emotions and aware of the emotions of others, learning to separate the two. As it becomes instinctive, we learn to value our own feelings and to recognize the feelings of others without being verwhelmed by them. As adults we then decide with whom we will or won't permit emotional intimacy.

- Mental Boundary – Third to form is our mental boundary, which lets us make decisions about the world. We learn instinctively to make up our minds from our own thoughts blended with the thoughts of those we share our intellectual intimacy with.

- Spiritual Boundary – The last to form is our spiritual boundary, which lets us decide who we will or won't share our psyche with. It is deeply influenced by our feelings about our place in the universe and the nature of its origin. When we have a healthy spiritual boundary we naturally feel a sense of self-esteem from knowing our place in the world. The people we share our spiritual intimacy with are the ones that we feel most comfortable around, without any need for secrets.

Sensing, Feeling, and Moving in the Body

Eurynome

from space I arose.
awake in the great nothing
that is all potential.
the great swirling field
the empty void of space
all that can be all that is...
my joy, so complete,
be-ing overcome with delight.
my body moved in ecstatic pleasure.
ripples of laughter bubbling forth,
I am lost in my intensity...
I dance forth creation
dividing earth and sky
dancing on the waves,
birthing the north wind
creating in my joy.
lost in my dance
I am all that is.

As human beings, our bodies are fully capable of being *sensing* bodies. We come into this world as infants, somatic in nature—all sensory awareness—without cognitive processes. We are *all feeling*. Our parents, in their care for us, serve as the cognitive part of our worlds until we reach a certain stage of our development—a time when we are able to move out of our full-body awareness into our cerebral functioning or thinking processes.

Some of us, out of pure need for survival, developed very quickly into thinking beings, leaving completely behind the somatic self, because it was not safe to be in the sensory body. Such people were in situations where thinking was necessary to survive.

Because so many of us grew up in troubled homes, we have few memories of being children. Many of us have very little awareness of being fully alive, fully expressive, and fully in our bodies. Many of us left our child-selves behind, but our task now is to retrieve her, to find that child of feeling, the one who experiences pleasurable sensation all throughout her body.

If we are to fully embrace living a magical life it is important to remember how to live in our bodies comfortably and safely. If we re-awaken all of our senses, our awareness is expanded and our perceptions clarify and develop. Without this, our magical life will not develop as it could. Our enjoyment of all that is Sacred will be impeded as if walled in and separated from all that is possible.

When I was a child and I needed to remove myself from what was threatening to me, I found solace in nature. I grew up near the Pacific Ocean and was, from an early age, like Child to Mother, fully attached to the Sea. Even today, just standing with my feet in

Her blessed waters, I am relieved of my sorrow and stress. Swimming in her, my body finds total freedom.

When I was no longer near the Ocean, I discovered trees. I climbed them to the highest places to rest my body on their branches and be comforted as no human ever comforted me.

And finally, when no escape was possible other than my room, I had my music. I have always used music to comfort, to heighten, or to fully experience any emotion that I might be having. As a child, I lay on my bed, the music playing next to me. I felt it course through my body much as I sense energy today, feeling it move, dancing it with my hands, all over my body.

Twenty years ago when I found Goddess I suddenly became aware how I had lost that sensing, feeling child and how much work I had in front of me to find, heal, and restore her. Now, so linear in my thought processes, so cut off from my ability to express emotion, feeling and yet unable to express, those feelings so long stifled within needed to be opened and embraced. I knew I had to find a way to get out of my head and back into my body.

And so I began a dedicated process of developing my sensory awareness. I first learned how to be visual, working very hard, practicing to see with my mind's eye anything I could dream of. I placed objects in front of me, looking at them and then closing my eyes to see them inside my head. I imagined how they might look on the side that I could not see. I practiced with all kinds of things and then began to create them in my head with my imagination.

After working with images of objects I began to pay very close attention to verbal descriptions in the books I read, stopping for a "check-in" to see what I had read in my mind. I invested in guided mediation tapes that took me on journeys allowing me to see all manner of things around me that would include seasons, people, and whole scenarios. I often found I would get way ahead of the spoken word in the meditation, my imagination was so active.

When I first began working with energy I used my inner vision to "see" energy as I moved it around in my Circles. I worked with my chakras, using color, breathing in and out each color and visualizing the spinning wheel at each center. I would fill my Circles with various colors, depending on what I wanted to do with my space.

All of these are different visualizing techniques. Experiment for yourself. Try a lot of different things. Each little success will lead you to another. The benefits of good visual skills will serve you well!

I also spent time connecting with my sense of smell. I played with herbs. I burned them one at a time hoping to discover how they affected me. Did I feel hot, cold, wet, sad, or joyful? What did they do to me when I smelled them? Without ever looking an herb up in a book, I would burn it and sit with it for a bit, sensing how I felt. Then I took notes so that when I learned to make my own incenses I could create something specifically for me. This would trigger my own senses rather than those claimed to be correct by some author of a book.

I noticed that my sense of taste seemed to be very developed (eating good food had always been a great pleasure). I pondered why I constantly craved spicy flavors over milder ones. Why did I always desire that full flavor? And so I played with tasting the more subtle flavors, taking time to fully explore and discover the rich underlying tastes and sensations. I spent time creating different taste combinations on my plate. I tried eating a taste of this and a taste of that from my plate. I then tried eating only one thing before moving on to the next. It was surprising to me what a difference it made by varying how I ate my food.

I listened to all kinds of music, observing the affect each piece had on me. What emotions came to me while listening? What memories were triggered? What did I feel before? How did I feel during? And how did I feel after hearing each piece? I learned that I could use music to enhance my moods or to change them. When I was sad, I could play sad music and really get into being very, very sad. But what I discovered was that by experiencing the feelings fully, I was able to move through and out of the sadness without any lingering effects.

Then one day...I discovered dance! I had forgotten the role dancing had once played in my childhood, the many years of dance lessons and stage performances—such an integral part of my childhood! How could I have forgotten what had once been so vital to me for so long?

With that, I began my practice of ecstatic dancing. When dancing returned to my life, I reconnected with my body, just like that! It was so easy. It was like coming home to a long lost friend.

When I do private ritual I always begin with the Dance. The Dance is what enables me to reach the trance state. The dance is how I now do most of my manifesting and private magical work

I began my practice of ecstatic dancing by listening to all types of music. I found that my body at times would want to move slowly, in dreamy, drifty ways, with an ease and gentle flow. I found flutes and violins wonderful for that less energetic form of dancing. I selected short pieces, not having any intention of dancing for long periods of time.

On occasion, I would have an opportunity at gatherings and festivals to participate in drum circles and celebrations around a fire. The urge would always arise to join with the dancers at the edge of the fire. Some people dancing around fires are often very active, moving about at great speeds in their dance. My needs seemed to be of a mellower variety. I would find my own spot and stay very close to the edge, looking directly into the flames, my gaze moving deeply into the embers. I would begin to feel the rhythm of the drums and become simultaneously one with the flames and the pounding of the drums, fully lost in my trance.

About this time I also discovered percussive world music and explored the work of such artists as Brent Lewis, James Asher, and Babatunde Olatunji's Drums of Passion. A whole new world of music opened for me! Then, recorded trance dance music became available in the work of Professor Trance and the Energizers and Gabrielle Roth. That is when I moved fully into ecstatic dancing. Their music comes to us recorded in one long continuous flow without track changing interruptions. Now available to me was a way to dance for long periods of time, experiencing changes in rhythms and various moods. Their music allowed me to deepen my experience of being one with the music.

Ecstatic dance is a wonderful way to retrieve the sensing, feeling girl-child you may have lost. To practice ecstatic dance, begin by selecting your music. Allow your feelings of the moment to help you select what is appropriate. Set aside some time when you can be alone, just you and the music. Wear something comfortable. I like dancing in a sarong, the rest of my body free to move. As the music begins to play, be still and allow the music to come into your body, gently observing how you feel and what thoughts come to mind. Notice what parts of your body are responding. Close your eyes and become a part of the sound. Allow your body to move where it will, easing into the dance, eyes closed, feeling, being, and one with the music. Remember, this is your dance. No one is watching. It is not about any practiced steps or patterns, but rather an adventure in how your body feels in response to what it hears. No one is watching. No one is judging. This is your own creation, one meant just for you. By keeping your eyes closed, you are removing yourself from one level of reality and moving into your own private place, where nothing exists other than you and the music. Connect with the rhythms. Become one, feel it flow within you as it moves through your body in waves and streams. Simply enjoy.

The Dance

A Sample Ritual using Dance

I place what I need on my altar: my stones, my Goddess images, water, salt, and my incense burner. My sacred flame is burning and has been burning this whole day. It's light reminding me of my work this night.

I have been dancing, dressed in my earth-tone sarong, deep orange, brown and green, bare breasted—dancing for Goddess, celebrating my beauty and the beauty of all women's bodies.

I begin by taking my incense, lovely patchouli, and with music loud and primal, I anoint my body while I dance the rhythms of my soul. I smell the essence of the wood, I feel it caress my skin—I am Air. I see the beautiful pink dawn of morning and feel the fresh clean air of Spring. I can feel life bursting forth. Off in the distance comes my hawk to join me in my sacred space. I dance with Air.

I am Air.

I turn to my altar once more, to my sacred flame, running my hands over and through the flame, over and over, feeling the warmth flickering on my skin. I am fire. I dance with Fire, taking the heat of the flame to my third eye, and ask that the spark be bright this night. Again, reaching into the flame I hold the heat to my heart and fill it with the warmth of love. Swelling— it feels strong and light, happy, loving the dance.

Once more my hands return to the flame and I feel the heat. I see it dancing with me in my song. I take the heat to my belly chakra, bringing the creativity of my passion—bringing it alive this night! I turn and dance around the room, spirited and alive, loving the dance, loving being in my body. I feel the music moving within me as my own energy, wild and free, pulsing with the rhythm—ready to make my magic come to me now.

Again I return to my altar, now placing my hands in the bowl of water. I wash my face, running my hands lightly down the skin of my neck to my breasts— feeling their woman's fullness, nipples stiffening as pleasure comes to me in the touch. Then down to the belly, swaying with the music—alive to the dance within.

Water...I become water. I feel the fluids of life where I once carried my babies in the womb. Then at once, I am in the water, first riding the wave of the ocean—reveling in the speed of my body moving with the waves. I am then in a cascading waterfall—showered in newness and beauty, fresh and clean!

I dance once more to my altar and reach for the salt. I sprinkle it upon me and around altar, across and around the room—feeling its grounding power. I place a bit of it upon my tongue, thanking the Earth for Her bounty. I take my crystal from the altar and once more dance around the room, holding the crystal in my dance, feeling alive and vibrant—lost in my dance.

My sacred space now created, I take my place before my altar, breathing in the smell of patchouli and hearing the music. I feel my heart pound with the sound, feel the pulse of the music filling me and coursing through my body. I am one with this place. I am one with the music and the energy I have created here NOW. I am Goddess, joyful, strong and beautifully alive in this moment. I am truly here now.

My work is before me so I breathe in the air around me, feeling it enter through my nostrils, filling my lungs, my breath—the clean, sweet air shared with all that is. And then, I let it go, relaxing in my breath in and out. I breathe slowly and surely, centering myself and feeling at peace.

I am ready, and I begin! Loudly, I shout to the world, to the Elements, to all powers that are, and to the Universe. What is mine by right comes to me now. All that I desire...manifesting now.

I shout again, and again. A powerful magic is taking place. I repeat again, but this time a bit softer, and then again softer still. And again...and again, until I reach a whisper, and then only in my mind's voice. Taking a few more deep breaths, I am still, the words repeating over and over in my mind. Slowly, I rise. I turn to the East and speaking clearly, once more say my words. I turn to the South and I say them again. I turn to the West, again, say my words, and then to the North, placing my hands flat-together on my altar. Facing North, I look to the Old Ones, I smile. I have tears in my eyes, because I know—it is Done!

The next day I will take my papers, left for now, on my altar. I will burn them in the morning and take a walk on the beach, releasing the energy to the birthing sea. For I have, indeed, birthed my desires this night.

Questions to ask yourself and suggestions for things to do:

What are some of your favorite smells? Are there herbs that you like better than others? When you wear perfumes do you like the sweet ones, fruit scents, musky odors, or spicy?

When you smell certain things, do you suddenly have memories associated with those smells?

What scents would you like to have in your sacred space?
What are your favorite flavors? Do you like spicy or sweet, salty or tart? Are there some foods that are "comfort" foods for you?

Do you consider yourself a visual person? Try some visualization for yourself and record your findings. Try listening to a guided meditation tape. Were you able to "see" what the artist was describing?

What affect does music have on your emotions?

Experiment with different types of music. Also record in your journal how you feel before listening to a particular piece. Record how you feel while listening, and again how you feel after.

Is there a certain type of music that encourages your body to move?
Are you comfortable with dancing? Are you able to be at ease, allowing your body to feel music and move with it?

Set aside a time to experiment with music and dance. Have a clear space with no one else around. Create an environment that no outside influence or other person can inhibit you in your dance.

Close your eyes as the music begins. Stand, breathe and feel the music. Let the music take form—feel its shape, see its color. Allow the music to be like a moving energy. Music is vibration, so try to feel the vibration and flow of energy as it enters and moves through your body. If you like, you can even use your hands to move this flow.

Just be in the moment. Don't worry if your body only moves a little, and don't be concerned about how you might look. No one else is there. No one can see. This is about feeling, not seeing.

Record your thoughts, feelings, and comments in your journal about this experience.

Living a Magical Life

In previous chapters, we have learned about Goddess, the Elements, creating sacred space, and how to cast our circles. We are now ready to explore magic and the power to be co-creators in our own lives.

I chose to place the study of the Elements, as well as the chapters on creating sacred space and casting circles, earlier in the book because I feel they are necessary to learn before approaching magic. I like to work magic within sacred space, in a self-created container. That is not to say that magic is to be used only for creating sacred space or circles. Nor does one have to cast a circle in order to do magic. Sacred spaces, as well as contained circles, have many uses such as meditation, healing, private devotion, contemplation, and sometimes as a place to just sit and rest the soul. In this chapter we will discuss magic and its application. We will discuss the concepts, ideas, and ingredients of working magic. In the next chapter I will share with you a step-by-step process, a practical application of the work. I will also provide you with many correspondences that are useful in magical work. We will explore the use of stones, herbs, oils, colors and candles, as well as some astrological and lunar applications. All of these things are very helpful in producing desired outcomes.

With my child's-eye view of the world, everything is magic. Truly, I will never understand how or why everything in life happens. I do know that I am always amazed at the wonder of it all. It is all magic; the sun comes up every morning, the moon rises, my new born child taking his first breath, feeling the raw power of a giant ocean wave crashing into the boulder at my feet, holding my arms around a giant redwood tree in the Sequoia's, and watching zillions of small ants as they all respond to any threat to their mound...it is all magic.. Knowing that I am one with all of this is amazing. All of life is magic. I will never know how it all works, but knowing that we simply are, that life is, that this universe exists, is magic.

This is all magic that occurs outside my intent. What I would like to explore here is the process of creating, through the use of magic, for the purpose of fulfilling one's desires and needs.

I know that I am one with all of creation. I am one with Goddess. I know that I can co-create, and manifest into my life, all of my desires. I can co-create what is right for me because of this *Oneness*.

Since the beginning of time, people have practiced magic. There have always been those who know what plant allies to use, or how to work with *devas* (unseen spirits), present in all of life. For thousands of years, there have been people who know how to work with the energies of life in practicing magic. The ingredients are simple. For me, magic is recognition that I am one with the web of life, a co-creator in my own path, and that I can manifest my desires. I can do this through an active use of my mind—my imagination, my creative energy, and the energy of my kin (all of the web of life).

The mind is a wonderful thing. The mind, with directed intent, fueled by the energy of the body and working in harmony with nature, can make magic happen. It is in my mind that imagination takes place. I use my imagination to visualize my goal. I see myself being or having my stated desire. I believe in the reality of an unseen world and know that what I have created in my mind with my imagination is now real. I may only be able to see it in my mind's eye, but I know that—as a form of thought—it is real. It will manifest into the "world of form" when I add my creative energy, as well as the energy of those things found in nature that are working with me.

I won't say that, just because you create an image in your mind that it will always manifest into something for you. I know that it *is* possible; however, I also know that by working with nature, it is a powerful partnership. Working with plant and stone helpers, the trees, animal friends, and the earth beneath my feet, and in harmony with all of these things, I will benefit greater and quicker rewards than using only my own generative fire.

How do we create our desire within our minds? First, we visualize it. We imagine it. We see what it is we want in our mind's eye. We focus within and allow this image to emerge, molding it to suit, getting it to look just as we want it to look. Once we can see it, we have created it! It is real! It is a part of us and we can allow ourselves to identify with it. This is our creation! If you are not visual, you can learn to be, but you can also use your body's other senses. You can *feel* yourself as you desire to be, or also hear words in your mind stating your desire.

In addition to creating an image, a thought within our minds, we must also generate a passion for that which we wish to manifest. Our emotions play a key role in our magical work. Our desire, our love, our will—these feelings make our magic strong.

Another ingredient in magic is working with our kin in the web of life. Gifts are given freely so long as we use them harmoniously. When I work magic I call on the Elements of Air, Fire, Water, and Earth to aid me in my work. I think of these as the Mother's First Children. I may work with a tree branch, choosing an appropriate tree for my work, and, as I do in my lunar rituals, I ask the tree's blessing. I use essential oils made from plants whose energies are known to be useful for my purpose. I select colors with properties specific to the work I wish to do. I might ask a stone to help me in my work, and I may light a candle as a visual symbol—as a focus or visual reminder of the work I am doing.

All of these things are available to me because we are all part of the same Whole. Their energy is freely given. My energy is also available to them as we are connected in life, and I freely give. I honor all of them as related to me and we work together. When I knew, really knew I was one with All That Is, I learned how to apply what I already knew to combine it with my new knowledge to work with all of my helpers, actively co-creating. With them, using my own creative power as well, we weave like a spider, creating a wondrous web all for the highest good.

The language of magic is full of symbols and images. Symbols and images trigger memories within us, hold our focus, and allow us to reach deeper levels of our unconscious mind. They bridge the gap in our awareness and allow both sides of our brains to work in harmony. They evoke feelings as well as intellect. We use shapes, colors, objects, scents and images to enhance our work. What is close at hand often works the best.

Learning the craft of magic involves learning how to relax, how to use imagination, and how to focus energy. Each time you create a simple magical-working you are developing your skills. Practice, practice and more practice!

One might ask, how is magic different for women? First of all, as explained in a previous chapter, if you view all life as whole, as one web, we call that web—as ordered by some power—Goddess. We acknowledge Her as all energies, not divided, and not dualistic. And yet, She is also many, since all that she has created is also *Her.*

What makes our magic different in our role as women who honor Goddess as Source? As we identify with Goddess, as parts of *Her* and goddesses ourselves, we have within our own creative power-center an ability to create and manifest. As women, we use that power-center to fuel our intent. Our energy is raised from this place, our creative center, which we also call our "womb" center. It is located below the navel, in the area of the second chakra. As women, we build and project our power from this spot within our bodies. That is the final piece of the puzzle, which, added to all the rest, fuels our energy and adds to the creative life force of our work.

It is also possible to work magic from other energy centers in the body and working with them can be very interesting. I would recommend learning about the chakras and the energies that are produced in each. Once familiar with them, directing energy from them in magical application produces interesting results. I especially like using heart chakra energy, using it almost exclusively in my healing work.

Those of us who practice magic have learned that we must be scrupulously honest in all areas of our lives. Magic works on the principle that says, "It is so because I say it is so." As a result, my word is important. What I say must be true and my word never broken. I must understand my own personal power. It must be a part of my life in all ways, in practical application and in magical application.

And finally, there is a question of ethics. Ethics, if you think about it, are deeply personal. Often, perception from one person to the next differs. As in all things, and magic is no different, we must each examine for ourselves, the ethics of any situation we face.

Whatever we choose to do, always think of Newton's Third Law of Motion—for every action there is an equal and opposite reaction. Weigh heavily all acts against this law.

Whether you believe in karma or not, physical laws, proven physical laws are in place. Look to your ethics and determine for yourself where you apply your energy, be it in an everyday act or in a magical act. You are responsible for your actions and all consequences.
I invite you now to begin your exploration of the world of magic. Next you will learn about working magic to start you on your magical path. Have fun! Learn the delightful combination of serious work and pure play.

We have already discussed the concepts behind magic. Now, we will explore ideas and ways to create magical workings using symbols and various objects, as well as some wording you might like to experiment with. The idea is to get you started. Once you have the idea, the best magic comes from your own creative mind.

Working with magic is not a complicated procedure. It is extremely easy to understand. All that is necessary are your "ingredients," positive thoughts, and your own creative energy. Through your own concentration, imagination, and determination, you direct your thoughts toward your desired objective in a positive manner. The more you visualize what it is you are achieving, the more it becomes a manifested reality, and in turn that reality will become fully realized in the world of form, as you have seen it. Add to that the help of other available energies and you will have all that you need to co-create.

The following information is to help you with ideas that, coupled with your own intuition and imagination, will create your own special magic! Know that in all magical work, you can be as simple or as complicated as you desire. All that is required is an active use of imagination, the purity of your intent, your energy, and that of any helpers you use.

When I decide I wish to work with magic in achieving a desired goal, I have certain steps that I follow in the preparation ad creation of my magical act. Outlined here are some basic steps and questions you may refer to later:

Decide, what is the purpose of the work? Is my work to be manifesting, repelling, or containing (a binding protective work).

What is the goal? Is it to manifest something into form or to cast something away from me? Or, is it a shielding of some kind?

At this point, I look at my desired goal and examine it from every angle, making sure that my work affects only me and is not a manipulative act. Not that I would ever do magic that *is* manipulative...I just prefer to choose my own battles, honoring Newton's Third law—I weigh heavily the price I might pay should I attempt this kind of magic.

Now, how will I do the work? What magical tools do I have that I can use in my work? These could be wands, blades, images, and visual symbols. What materials will I use? Do I wish helpers from the plant or mineral kingdoms to aid me? Do I want to use herbs, make incense, use oils, or make a sachet? If I wish to make an item in this working, what materials will I need on hand to create it? Should I pay attention to *when* I do this work? Is it important to look at astrological influences? Do I need to do the work on a particular phase of the moon? Is there a time of day that would be best, and do I need to consider what day of the week on which to do my work?

What do I wish to say in my work? What should be my stated purpose, my intent, and my desired goal? What energies would I like to have present in my work? Is there a special Goddess that I wish to be with me? How will I invite all of this into my space? How will I thank them, say good-bye, and close down the Circle?

Will I raise energy in this work? Will I sing, chant, dance, use special gestures, or would I prefer to use meditation as a tool for my work? If I do wish to raise energy, from where in my body do I wish to direct its flow? Will I use my visual skill seeing its movement and increase, or will my body be the instrument and feel it as it builds around me? Will I give it color or temperature? What will be its texture?

What other symbols and sensory-aids will I want to use? Should I use candles, and if so, what colors?

Will I inscribe my candles? Will I anoint them? Charge them? And if so, how will I do that? Do I wish to use any other object or image to serve as a visual symbol in my work?

Having written all of that down, I will have formulated the process I will use. I will be ready to do an act of magic!
Now that you have a checklist, I'd like to walk you through a working, following the steps one-by-one together.

Suppose I am a student, and in a few days I will have to take a test which will determine my final grade for the semester. I want to use magic to help me pass this test. First of all, before we get into the magical aspect of passing the test, as far as I am concerned I will not be assisted by any of my allies, nor will the universe be very supportive of my work if I don't do my part. That means that I still need to study. I still need to apply myself to the task in this visible *world of form*. That being said let us look at the work ahead.

So, what is the purpose of the work? Is my work manifesting, repelling or containing?

The stated purpose is to make an excellent grade on my test. So, the work is manifesting work.

What is the goal? Is it to manifest something into form or to cast away? Or, is it a shielding of some kind?

The work is to manifest an excellent grade on the test. This is manifesting in the world of form, bringing it in.

At this point, I look at my desired goal and examine it from every angle, making sure that my work affects only me and is not a manipulative act. I weigh heavily the price I might pay should I attempt this kind of magic.

I can clearly see that my getting a good grade on a test in no way has any affect on anyone else. I am not manipulating another in my desire.

How will I do the work?

I wish to do my work within sacred space in the form of a ritual.

What magical tools do I have that I can use in my work? This might be wands, blades, images, and visual symbols.

I would like to create an altar. I would like to have a visual symbol before me of the desired result. I will need to create what will look like test results, with the grade showing (like a report card). I can create this easily with pen and paper. I would like to have a candle that will represent my clarity of thought and intellectual success. For that I will choose a yellow candle. I will use a taper candle so that I can anoint it with oil. I will need the things I usually have on my altar—my blades, symbols of each of the elements, a

Goddess candle, in addition to the other things listed below.

What materials will I use? Do I wish helpers from the plant or mineral kingdoms to aid me? Do I want to use herbs, make incense, use oils, or make a sachet? If I wish to make an item in this working, what materials will I need to create it?

I would like to create a talisman in my Circle to carry with me when I take my test. This talisman will be a small bag that will fit in my pocket so that I can reach in and hold it when I need to find clarity in my thought processes while I am taking the test. In this bag I think I will place a stone. I will select purple fluorite octahedron for its known association to mental clarity and inner vision. I will put a small amount of sage for clearing away any negativity that may be around me at the time. I will also want a small amount of mugwort to help fine-tune my mind's ability. I have a buckeye that I think will also be great to have in it. (Buckeyes are known to bring good luck.) I will additionally need a small piece of fabric. I think it might be nice to use purple for spiritual power, and I will also use a gold cord (for success) to tie it. I will wish to use some incense while doing my work. I think I will use simple, amber incense, calling on the wisdom of the Old Ones to help me in my work. And finally, I need an oil to anoint my candle. I like the idea of honeysuckle, which is perfect for mind clearing, studies, and success.

What should I pay attention to when I do this work? Is it important to look at astrological influences? Do I need to do the work on a particular phase of the moon? Is there a time of day that would be best? And, do I need to consider what day of the week on which to do the work?

Since I have to take this test in three days time, I think I will do the work the night before I take the test. I don't think it is an issue of needing the right phase of the moon, or astrological help. The immediacy says doing it right before the test will get the best results.

What will I wish to say in my work? What will be my stated purpose, my intent, and my desired goal? What energies would I like to have present at the work? Is there a special Goddess that I wish to be with me? How will I invite all of this into my space? How will I thank, say good-bye, and close down the Circle?

I will need to create a statement about my desire. Even if I don't say the statement out loud, I do need to have it clear in my mind. So let's try saying this, "With the use of clear intellect and proper preparation, success is mine in achieving excellent scores on my test." I will invite each of the Elements to assist me in my work as well as invoking Minerva, who is the Goddess of Wisdom, into my Circle.

Will I raise energy in this work? Will I sing, chant, dance, use special gestures, or would I prefer to use meditation as a tool for my work? If I do wish to raise energy, from where in my body do I wish to direct its flow? Will I use my visual skill, seeing its movement and increase, or will my body be the instrument and feel it as it builds around me? Will I give it color or temperature? What will be its texture?

I think in this working, after the positive affirmation has been stated, the candle dressed and lighted, the visual of a successful grade report created, and all these visuals are present as I create my talisman, the energy will be quite sufficient. When I have made the bag, I will bless it with each of the four elements, and sit within, meditating, pouring my energy and thoughts into it to be used when I take the test.

What other symbols and sensory-aids will I want to use? Do I want candles, and if so, what colors? Will inscribe my candles? Will I anoint them? Charge them? And if so, how will I do that? Do I wish to use any other object or image to serve as a visual symbol in my work?

I think I covered all of this above. But it is always important to take a last look to make sure I have thought of everything. I will then write everything down. I will have formulated the process I will use. I will be ready to do an act of magic! Here's what I might write:

In two days time, when darkness has fallen, I will cast my Circle and do this work. Between now and then, I will be studying in preparation for the test. The morning of the test, I will put my charged talisman (the bag) into my pocket, feeling confident and assured of success.

I mentioned earlier the process of anointing a candle. This is also called "dressing" a candle. This is the name we use for the process of applying the oil to the candle. Not only do you apply the oil, as you put it on the candle you also begin the process of thinking, visualizing your intent and actually infusing the candle with that intent. When using a taper candle, place a small amount of oil in the palm of your hand. Rub your hands together and place both hands in the center of the candle. Holding the candle with one hand, rotate your hand around the candle, dispersing the oil around the candle. And, moving your hand at the same time, continue doing this all the way to the end. Then coming back to the center, now hold the candle with your moving hand and do the same movements with the other hand. Be sure to focus on the work at hand, seeing your outcome in your mind's eye.

Working with herbs to use as incense

It always compliments the work to create incense specifically for your work. If you are unable to do this there are many incenses and herbs available for your use.

If you have never made herbal incense before, or have never burned specific herbs for specific magical work, the very best way to learn is to spend time with each herb.

Get yourself a special cauldron (a fireproof container that will be safe to burn charcoal in). Special charcoal is available for burning herbs. I like to put either sand or kitty litter (of which I always have a liberal supply) in the bottom under my charcoal to absorb the heat.

Select about five herbs each time you do this, as burning more at any one sitting will be difficult. Our noses become desensitized after introduction of too many scents.

Get your charcoal burning. While it gets itself ready, ground, center and focus your attention on the work at hand. When the charcoal is ready, place a small amount of the first herb on top. Sit with the smell. Then sense how you feel. Do you notice any thoughts, feelings, or emotions arising? Are you feeling hot, cold, or clammy? Are there any memories that come to you while sitting with this herb? Herbs will tell you how they are to be used when calm and centered, when open to any form of communication from them. In your journal, record the name of the herb and anything you might have experienced. When you have completed your work with this herb, select the next and repeat this process.

Certainly you can buy a book and read what herb might work for many different things, but the key in any magical working is *what does that herb do for you*? The only way to discover this is by experimentation. What someone else says may not apply to you at all. You are your own best teacher.

Keep your notes. Continue experimenting with herbs. At some point you might decide to create special incense for a specific occasion. You can look through your notes and combine those herbs that evoke certain feelings in you that you wish to include in your magical work.

This is really fun work! I remember when I first started; I still had kids at home, but they were really adult-kids or young adults, and I could hear them downstairs moaning and groaning, "What's Mom burning now?" But these same kids later came to me for magical advice in their own work!

Now just for fun... a bit of hair braiding magic. If you are feeling a bit timid, uncertain or have to make an appearance somewhere that you may not be totally comfortable about, this wonderful little "spell" is very effective. This is for a special type of empowerment, especially if you have long hair! Braid your hair into as many small braids as you like—you can do them under your hair where they don't show or on top. You don't have to do all of your hair, just enough to give you that Celtic Warrior look! While braiding, chant the following!

Braid the Magic
Braid the spell
Hold the thought
That all is well.

Warrior Braids do
Braid the charm
Twisting evil
Bending harm.

Braid the Will
Make it strong
Return to sender
Any wrong

Warrior Braids
Make the spell
Wrapped in love
All is well.

I guarantee you will arrive where you are going feeling strong and brave and sure!

Questions to ask yourself and suggestions for things to do:

Take some time to think about ethical values. What are yours?

Where in your life does magic apply? Do you see how being able to become a magical person in every area might be life-enhancing? Record in your journal how becoming a magical person could affect you and how you live your life.

Become this new magical person by creating one positive image for yourself for the day. If you know what your day has in store for you, take time at the beginning to see yourself just as you wish to be. If you want to feel joyful, build that joy inside as you start your day. Smile internally, as big as you can. Think of the things in your life that bring you that joy. Hold those within your image of yourself as you move through the day.

Plan to do a magical working. It can be a healing. It can be to manifest one small thing within yourself, perhaps in the way you view a situation that you would like to change—so that you feel better about it.

What helpers will you choose to aid you in your work? What symbols will you select to help you?

Explore the chakras. Learn what each energy center represents. Learn to use color and sound to magnify, clear, and balance each chakra.

Record your thoughts of this work in your journal, and as you write, begin to think how you would make this change happen. Create a small ritual to make this change.

Create a small candle working. Write down all of your thoughts and preparation steps in your journal. First decide what the work is. Then begin to think about what candles to use.

What colors, oils, or astrological symbols? Create a working. Think clearly about your intent and outcome. Examine whether this is a working that is not manipulating another.

Look at what you want to accomplish from every angle. Create the words you will use, possibly as short poem that can be chanted over and over as you build energy. Perhaps you will have certain words just in your head. Consider though that stating or shouting out loud is very effective—if you are alone this is perfect. If others are in your house, it is not as easy to be so verbal.

Choose what time of day to do the work. Examine the phase of the moon and select an appropriate time.

When it's the right time, do your working. Remember to visualize and see the outcome as you work. When using plants, stones, and other helpers, be sure to give thanks.

Record everything in your journal that might occur while you work. Write down thoughts feelings, and results.

Working With Crystals and Gemstones

This chapter introduces a very personal method for working with crystals and gemstones. It will include getting acquainted, clearing, and enhancing. The emphasis is on personal sensing and feeling, rather than what the "experts" tell you. This chapter will help you develop a relationship with the *deva* within each stone, as well as introduce you to the concept of the transmutation of energy.

Imagine that a rock you are holding in your hand is the home of a very small, invisible deva. This little deva is very old, as old as the Earth Herself. Because this small deva is so very old, it is also very wise—filled with the wisdom of the Earth. This deva is a child of the Mother, just as we are children of the Mother, and only wishes to serve in whatever capacity it may, so long as the service is also in accordance with the Mother's wishes. Remember, we are all one with the Web of Life.

Now, I won't tell you that you have to believe the deva is there. If you don't believe that it is, then for a moment, just for a moment, simply suspend your disbelief, for the purpose of working with the stone.

As you hold the stone in your hand, send a thought into it, to the small deva, just to say hello and then tell it that you wish to share conversation with it for a while. Be very still; calm yourself down into a very relaxed state, focusing your attention on the stone in your hand. Be aware of any feelings you might have, thoughts that come into your mind, anything at all that might be perceived as a message from the deva. Notice how the stone feels in your hand. Is it warm, cold, prickly, smooth? Are you feeling happy, sad, joyful, angry, peaceful, excited, fidgety, or anxious? Just notice and feel.

Each little deva within a stone has a very special purpose, just as we do. If the deva is to help us with something, it helps to have the correct one for the job. We can very often narrow down our choices by choosing the appropriate color. These devas are drawn to a color that corresponds with their purpose, as they resonate with their own color and it enhances the work they do.

So, the first thing we want to find out from the deva in the stone is *what is its purpose*? Ask it. You don't have to speak out loud. You might feel very foolish in doing that. Simply thinking the question works. Listen for an answer. Open your heart to the deva. Allow it to speak with you.

Once you have determined its purpose, our next task is to find out how we might help the deva to better perform its function. How might we do that, you ask?

Let's do some imagining again. Remember when I said that the rock is a home for a very small deva? Well, all homes get dirty. Yours does, mine does, the deva's does as well. If we clean our house, we feel better and can do what we need to do inside it better. I never could cook in a dirty kitchen. Can you?

So what we have to do is help the deva clean up his house. He didn't get it dirty, life did. If we want to stay very clean physically and mentally, then from time to time we need to take a bath! We also clean ourselves mentally or psychically as we need to. Life just kind of gets in us and on us, especially other people's energies, some of which we really don't want hanging on to us any longer than necessary.

So, the first thing we do is ask the deva to send out all the dirt in his house to us. Ask him to release it to you. Ask him to send it out so that it can collect on the palms of your hands. See the dirt coming out. Watch the dirt coming out until you can no longer see it. Now it is all collected on your hands. Yuck!

Now for the fun part!

We are going to use the natural energies of the Earth to transmute this dirt on our hands into useful energy. We don't just want to brush it off and let something else pick it up, do we?

First, allow the dirt to rise up off your palms into a cloud about one foot above them. See all the particles arise and form this cloud. See the dark, swirling cloud. Pull the energy of the Earth up through your feet into your hands and out the palms of your hands into the cloud. See the energies of the Earth swirl around with the particles of dirt.
Next pull the energy of the sun and sky down into the cloud. Watch this bright golden light enter the cloud,

mix with the energy of the Earth, getting lighter, and lighter, and lighter until it is a clear light golden ball of energy. When it reaches that point gently push it up and out to enter the universe as it will. WOW!

Now, back to our little deva; together you and she have cleaned her house, but all the work that she naturally does might have depleted her energy somewhat, so the next step is to ask the deva how you can help to replenish her energy so that she might better serve in her purpose. The energy needed is always going to include one or more of six things: energy from the four elements of air, fire, water, and earth, and of course, Goddess energy from the Great Mother Herself, which we can pull from the Earth, Sun, Moon, and Sky.

Listen to the deva and determine what you can send into the rock to help her. If it is difficult to determine exactly, it will always help to send a good balance of all energies. But first listen and see if you can tell what it needs. When you have studied and worked with the Elements, this part will become much easier. Because you know the energies of the elements you will also quickly intuit what the deva needs.

In addition to the energies mentioned above, other things could be sent in to help. They might include colors, music, sounds, thoughts, whatever you determine is necessary. Let your imagination play—that's what it's for!

When you are finished, ask again if there is anything else the deva needs. Listen and do what you can if there is more. Then ask the deva one last time if she has everything she needs. If the answer is finally yes, you now have a stone ready for work!

If you are going to be working with stones in your spiritual practice it is a good idea to have your very own set. If you truly love rocks you will eventually have quite a collection. Do the above with each stone in your collection so that you are intimately aware of each stone's purpose. It is a good idea to replenish the deva's home periodically and certainly after each use, especially when used in healing. Keep your stones in a special place of honor and smudge them occasionally (they love it!). It helps also to give them baths—good old soap and water! Take them out for visits often. They don't like neglect. If you care for them properly, you will be friends forever!

Questions to ask yourself and suggestions for things to do:

Do you already have a collection of rocks, gemstones and minerals? Do you have favorite crystals?

If so, take some time to clean each one. If they haven't had a good soap and water bath lately, give them one! Bring them back to sparkling clean!

Set aside some time each day to work with a stone or crystal. Get to know each one. Write your thoughts and feelings in your journal. What does each stone tell you about itself? How might you use it to enhance your life or that of another?

How might you help the stone or crystal to do its job more effectively? What does it need from you?

Become friends with your rocks and crystals. They are wonderful helpers, quietly working all the time as they share space with us.

Connecting with Our Kindred

All of creatures of The Mother are your kindred. The more you get to know other species, the more in tune you will be with your own energies, making you more able to walk in this world as a witch.

Begin by taking notice of the trees, plants, grasses, birds, and animals in your own neighborhood or nearby park. I like to have my journal with me so that if I want to make sure to remember something I can take note to explore it later.

When you take a walk, look at everything around you and greet all of The Mother's children warmly. You can do this silently in your mind and within your heart rather than risk being thought as totally nuts!

If you choose to connect with the trees, each time you pass by them, notice the changes in the growth and color of their branches, leaves, flowers, and fruit as the year turns. Also notice more subtle changes of mood and energy. Smile at them and touch them as you pass. Sit beneath a tree to eat your lunch, have an afternoon nap, or relax after work. Let the lives of trees become a part of your experience of your immediate world.

Connect with the grasses of your area. Lie upon them, feel their blades, smell their essence. Get to know the plants, their leaves, flowers, and berries. What can they tell you about themselves? What can you learn about them?

Do you see bees, butterflies, spiders, and ants? Notice where you see them, how they are living, what they are doing.

Look up. What birds are in the sky around your home? Do you feed them in your yard? What songs do they sing? Who do they get along with and from whom do they flea? What time of day do they sing the loudest and when are they the quietist? When are they most apt to feed?

Getting to know a tree is a very special kind of adventure. To begin a relationship with a tree, choose one that seems to be calling to you and move closer to it. Observe every part of it from root to top. Every tree has its own energy field. See if you can detect where it begins by walking toward and away from the tree, using the palms of your hands to sense its energy.

Send loving energy toward the tree from your heart, and ask if it will allow you to draw closer and spend some time with it. If it is granted, walk closer to the tree and walk slowly around it if you can. Place your hands, and perhaps your whole body, against the trunk and feel the tree's essence. Look at the tree to see how it looks up close. Pay attention to how it smells and feels against your skin. Is there a leaf nearby? Rub the leaf or needle between your fingers and inhale the fragrance.

Now sit down against the trunk and open yourself to the power of the tree. Let it take you into a deep state of relaxation. Be present with the tree, and likewise accept the presence of the tree; allow it to calm and gently cleanse your mind of all the agitation of the day. As you sit with this tree, ask it if there is a story it wishes to share with you. Then sit and just be with the tree. Observe your thoughts and feelings as you listen for any information that may come your way.

When you are ready, stand up and place your hands on the tree, sending a heartfelt thank you. Gratitude extended to the tree is an important part of building a relationship with it. It is a giving and receiving relationship that will endure through time.

Meditation

I believe one of the most difficult aspects of living a magical life is setting up the schedule and sticking to the discipline of a daily meditation practice. Let's face it, most of us lack discipline in our personal lives. We live with enforced "musts" and "shoulds" in every other part of our lives. So when it comes down to our precious personal time, of which most of us have so little, adding another discipline, yet another "should or must" is very hard for us.

And what makes it even worse, the practice of meditation is for the most part, boring! When we are new to the art, we think something miraculous is suppose to happen to us, that we "should" achieve some blissful, spiritual state that will bring us joy and a desire to continue experiencing such states.

Well, that isn't what happens! We go into a meditation expecting to be able to still our minds, to accomplish some great things for ourselves. When in fact, what happens is everything we need to be doing, everything we might want to plan or think about enters our mind, all the way down to that sandwich we suddenly are craving! The human mind is always "on." Even when we sleep, our minds are busy, busy, busy!

When I first decided I wanted to start meditating, I took my whole family to the TM Center and all of us were initiated into the art of transcendental meditation, complete with personally chosen mantras (even my children). A mantra is a specially selected sound. Now, they might mean something to someone who speaks Sanskrit, but to me they were simply sounds, and as such, evoked no particular associations or thoughts within myself. I was told to think the mantra, perhaps even see it floating through my mind, that I should hear it within, not with my ears. I was told to keep it internal and to never say it out loud. I was instructed to be gentle on myself; if I found myself suddenly thinking of something other than my mantra, I was to gently come back to the mantra, not to allow guilt or pressure.

TM was a pretty good way for me to meditate. I was successful for many years. It was not always easy because sometimes, frankly I was either not in the mood or I was in an easily distractible place. I came to realize with time and daily practice that 90% of my time was spent gently reminding myself to come back to my mantra and to relax. For that other 10% I would lose any awareness of thought processes. Periods of stillness of the mind…that was the ultimate goal to reach, however briefly.

The first thing to understand about meditation is, *why does one wish to meditate*? The idea is to develop methods of becoming still, ways to go within, and ways to open energy channels throughout the body. And as a result, we open our senses up so that we might experience life with our "whole" selves. The result of a good meditation practice is an enhanced awareness, a greater capacity of creativity, and more access to right brain functions. And at the same time, we become more fully "in the now" which allows us to accomplish more within our lives.

TM is only one way to do all of this. When I wanted to try other methods, it was hard for me because I had been practicing with TM for 12 years. My first experiments were with guided visualizations. There are some very good ones available on any subject you can imagine. And they serve an excellent purpose. What I found, however, was that the results I had with TM were not achieved using guided visualizations. What guided meditation was however, was an excellent method for developing inner sight and visual skill.

In the mid-80's I began a course of study within a system of Taoist Spiritual Alchemy. This too was excellent practice for me. It is a very visual system. For someone like me who must learn how to be visual, it was excellent! It was also wonderful practice for me because it is an emotional healing system. I am just recently beginning to explore it again using other techniques from other Taoist Masters, known to most as Qi-Gong.

Learning about the chakras and meditating on them can develop as an excellent practice. Chakras can be observed, cleared and enhanced though various techniques.

Somewhere along the way I discovered what is called Mindfulness Meditation, or by some, called a "sitting practice." Actually, this type of meditation is very similar to TM except there is no mantra. One may simply follow the breath—breathing in and out, being aware of the passage of air into the body and out. There's also the same gentle reminder if thoughts should interrupt the process. There is no strong focus, just awareness of the breath and simply being mindful of all that is present. It involves becoming still, allowing an observance without involvement in everything within our awareness.

From having tried many methods, I believe this type of meditation to be the most useful in giving our minds and our bodies a chance to slow down. Mindfulness can be practiced in many ways. It is not a meditation that you must sit still to do. I have had many a mindful walk, and never had I been more aware of the beauty around me. This type of meditation does bring us closer to our deep instinctual nature. It does allow us to "tune in" to our own wisdom. With practice every day (it's better if twice a day) we open to our spiritual nature and are able to reach deeply inside for the answers we need. It is not that we ask for this to happen in our meditations. It just simply does because of practice, but not necessarily while we are meditating. Often an answer will just enter our thoughts at some unexpected time later. It might even come to us in a dream.

Ecstatic Dance as Moving Meditation

Come fly with me
come on, come on, come
dance with me
come on, come on, come fly
come on and dance with me

Dance is a dynamic tool for awakening and stirring up the subtle forces and energies of life. It is an outer expression of an inner spirit. Dance and movement are natural to the universe. Plants will move gracefully to face the sun and wave in the breeze. Birds and animals display magnificent arrays of plumage and posture for everything from courtship to aggression. Dance is natural and vital to us as well.

We are all musical. We all have rhythm. Anyone can dance. We live in a time when we are too self-conscious and caught up with how we might look when we dance.

Ecstatic dance is a moving meditation—it is not a dance to do with someone else unless that's what you want. It is not a dance designed to "look" good. It is free flowing. It is aware. It is a dance between your spirit and the music.
How do you do it? Anyway you want! Anyway you feel the music. The idea is to let the music in, feel it, and then releases it through your movement. Whatever movement "feels" natural to you.

The choice of music is also up to you. There are many selections available that are designed to be used for movement, but you need to select what appeals to you.

Next, find a time that you can be undisturbed. Wear clothes that you like and feel good in, and that allow you to move comfortably; whatever appeals to you that will not restrict your movement. Clear an area. It does not have to be a large area because the dance is really happening within yourself. It is a good idea to be barefoot. I very seldom move my feet at all. It's about moving the body. Put on your music. Begin your movements slowly, warming up to the music. Breath naturally and easily, focusing on the music. Allow your body to seek a place in tune with what you feel. Get loose.

Begin to warm up by focusing on one body part. Say, first, your neck. Move it in time with the music. Get loose. Now, move your shoulders, your spine, your hips, and your knees. Continue focusing on different areas of your body until you have loosened up all over.

You should really be into your dance at this point. No one is looking. Free yourself. Become the music! Ideally, your ecstatic dance session should last at least twenty minutes. Most of mine last close to an hour.

When I first started ecstatic dancing, it was with a group of women. All of us wanted to experiment, so we wore blindfolds. By using blindfolds we were freed from the idea of someone looking at us. Amazing! You can't see anyone else, nor can they see you! This is not about how our dancing looks, but rather how it feels. Try it! Listen to the music. Act out how it makes you feel. Your imagination is a wonderful tool. Let it make pictures in your mind. Become the music. The first time we tried this, we danced for an hour—an hour of being completely unaware of anything but the music, our own minds and movements.

Ecstatic dancing comes more easily to some than others. It is particularly difficult for those of us who have allowed themselves to become slaves to time, machines, and consensus reality. Many of us have become victims of our left-brain logic and have stress-related disorders. If this describes you, as it did me, at least try ecstatic dancing. It is a great adventure and an opportunity to meet a part of yourself which has been dormant for a long time.

The ways and means for achieving altered states are many. Every culture around the world has developed many effective methods. Briefly, examples include Tai Chi, Qi-Gong, and shamanic journeying. Explore what works for you.

I cannot stress strongly enough that a meditation practice is essential to your spiritual development. Your journey will unfold in a better way. You will come to know yourself in ways never thought of before, and you will tap into your own Goddess Wisdom more fully as you walk through this life.

Questions to ask yourself and suggestions for things to do:

Decide for yourself what kind of meditation practice you would like to try first. Record this in your journal and any thoughts you might have about it. Commit to doing this practice twice a day for five minutes only.

After you have been able to do this each day, increase the time to ten minutes at each sitting. If you never do more than this for ten minutes, twice a day, this is excellent! More is even better, but you need to pat yourself on the back if you can maintain this accomplishment. It isn't easy.

Be sure to take time with your journal after each meditation, recording thoughts feelings and experiences. Also at other times of the day, record thoughts that occur, dreams that may come, inspirations, and any changes you might note once you have begun the practice of daily meditation.

Explore many different types of meditation. A student of mine decided to work on one form per month until she had tasted a variety and could determine for herself which was most beneficial to her.

Welcoming a Goddess

One of the most fulfilling aspects of being in tune with The Goddess and all of Her aspects is to come to know individual goddesses personally. Taking the time to do this has deepened my life experience and brought me a greater awareness of myself and the world around me.

There could be many reasons why I might wish to know a particular goddess better. It could be that she simply has been popping up in my reading. I may have read or heard her name and my curiosity level increased daily until I felt compelled to find out more about her. I may feel that she would be an appropriate aspect of The Goddess to call into my circle for a particular lunar cycle or magical working. I believe it critical to research a goddess before doing this, and better yet, really know who she is when you decide you would like to share sacred space with her.

And of course, there is the process of "aspecting" a goddess in ritual. Aspecting means that you not only invite a goddess to your circle, but she actually merges with you, bringing out who she is so that she may become visible to the others in the circle. She may even speak through you. She may talk to your sisters in circle. She may bring you a very special message while she is a part of you.

When I decide that I really want to know a certain goddess better, the first thing I do is research her. I find every resource available and I collect information about her. I read her stories. I find images to look at. I learn where she is from, why she is important, what her aspects are, who she loved, who her enemies were, and who worshiped her and why. I make copious notes and re-read them often, until I know everything there is to know about her. I will say that for some goddesses, I don't find a lot. I might find a sentence, or if I am lucky, a paragraph. For the more well-known ones, there is certainly much more to read and learn.

Once I have done this and I feel I have found all that I possibly can find, and when I feel that I have a pretty good grasp on who she is, I will invite her into my sacred space while in a meditative state. I do this by attempting to visualize her walking toward me. Or I may ask her, either out loud or in my mind, to please come and be with me for a while. I might read my information that I have collected on her. I may think of a song to sing that I think she will like. I may have written a poem about her, although the poems usually come after she has made herself known to me.

You might try seeing yourself in the place she is from. If, in your research you have come to love her, share that with her. Ask her to guide you. Let her know why you want to know her and open yourself so that she may come in.

The first time you call to her, you may feel as though nothing has happened. Don't be discouraged. You are creating a pathway for her. Perhaps you might view it as a bridge. Take it in stages, little baby steps. What normally happens is you begin to get "flashes". She may take form in your mind's eye, or she may speak to you. Don't worry if the images are unclear. You may not see anything if you are not a visual person. You may feel her presence instead, and sense how she is. Focus on how she comes to you. What do you see, what do you feel? Are their smells that come to your attention, feelings invoked, memories triggered? Can you see how she is dressed? Does she carry anything? Does she gift you with anything? Pay attention to how you feel, to any sensations or other realizations that come.

Be sure that when finished, when your time with her is concluded, that you thank her and remember to say goodbye. Ask her to please be there should you have a need or desire to call on her again.

I recommend that you repeat this process again, and again, until you find that she is there any time you call her to mind. In doing this, I have come to know my goddess well, so well in fact, that she seems to be a part of my consciousness and one with me, so that when I do wish to call her or ask for assistance, she is right there, as if she is a part of me. I always acknowledge her when she is present with me and I always show gratitude for her presence.

I have found through the years that the appearances of the goddesses I have worked with either slow down or speed up according to what is going on in my life. I have noticed that when one arrives, she is there for a particular for reason. I have trained myself to be very aware when a goddess appears to me unbidden. It is like a wake-up call. I explore very carefully what is happening in my life right at this moment so that I know why she is with me. I recognize that she has come to help in some way and I cannot ignore her choice to be with me at this time.

One thing of particular importance is that a goddess, once you have come to know her, may reveal to you that a particular story you have read about her is untrue. Many of the myths we read today are newer versions of her stories. Because her myths were written down at much later times than when her presence was known to women, and because her stories were written down during a time when she was no longer revered as the life-bringer, birthing, manifesting Goddess, she is often depicted in ways that are not true to her essence. She may reveal the truth to you. She may show you how the story really went. She may allow you to see how her story became twisted and what the story really means.

In my experience, when this happens the truth that she is trying to give me is of particular importance to women. If her original story was empowering to women, the odds are that it changed because the message was dangerous to the new power of patriarchy. So I ask that you pay very close attention if you gain new insights into her stories. They hold keys to your development. This is true whether you are male or female. It is important for us to know Her stories, in all Her aspects, as She originally told them to us.

Let me add something that I believe is very important. Because we revere Goddess as the Divine and call to Her as our Mother, this does not mean that we do not acknowledge that Her form contains both gods and goddesses, just as She has birthed males and females of many species. I invite you to explore Her sons as well.

There are both gods and goddesses in every culture around the world. As a Dianic practitioner it is very rare that I actually work with a god, but I have explored and gotten to know several when they seem to seek me. I check them out just as I would if a goddess is attempting to communicate with me. What I do find important in learning about the gods as well as the goddesses is in learning about their relationships. Knowledge of how they interact with each other is very valuable especially when applied to our relationships today. You are given a glimpse of beautiful and harmonious relationships between all aspects of Goddess.

My life is enriched by the presence of the goddesses I have chosen to work with. (My guess is that what I just said is totally backwards!) There are times that I know that they choose to work with me, that perhaps they called to me and needed to be known by me. I feel loved, protected, inspired, and made sacred by knowing them intimately. I am most grateful for their gifts.

Questions to ask yourself and suggestions for things to do:

Has an aspect of The Goddess been on your mind lately?

Who is she? Take time to research fully who she is. Write this in your journal. Ask yourself why she might be on your mind at this time.

Invite her into a meditation. Record any impressions, any messages, any gifts she might bring.

Do not be discouraged if it takes you several attempts. Be patient with yourself. Gently invite her each time. Notice small thoughts, feelings, and any sensations that you may have.

How might you now use the knowledge of her within your rituals? Can you think of ways you can share your knowledge of her with others?

Song and Chant

To be inspired—with words, song, dance or an art of any kind—is to breathe in, swim in, and to merge with the ways of the Muse. When you are truly inspired to sing, it's as if someone with an absolutely marvelous, powerful, perfect voice is singing through you. At the same time this feels like the "real you" that has been finally set free. You are, at last, giving the performance of your lifetime, doing what you have always longed to do, becoming totally *yourself*.

The KISS Principle ~ Keep It Simple Sister

For any group chant to be effective it must be simple enough for everyone to learn quickly. If the words to the chant are long and drawn out, and if those participating have not had ample opportunity to learn the words, then your chant will fall flat on its face and the group energy will also be scattered and flat. If you wish to raise a powerful energy within the group, all must be able to say or sing the words easily without thought, so that their minds can be focused on the energy and not the words. More simply, they must be able to get past trying to remember the words—it must be automatically coming out of their mouths. This way their thoughts will be only on group dynamics and power-building.

It is also not necessary that the vocals of a chant have to be words; they can be meaningless sounds. As an example, many Native American chants, whose words have no meaning for us at all, can be some of the most powerful chants in ritual. In Vedic Mantras and chants, the sounds come from what are called "seed sounds" that are believed to have a direct connection to the soul.

It is the group that builds the power of a chant, not any specific individual. Group chants are lead by someone, and it is the interaction between the group and that individual that builds an effective chant. The person leading the chant must stay attuned with the group and be able to sense the energy, involve everyone into the dynamics, and know when to raise, lower, build, and when to stop energy growth. The group is an orchestra with a conductor. Consequently, each musician must be observant of the conductor while the conductor must be focused on the whole as well as each individual musician.

Here are three different types of energy waves created in chant:

1. In starting a chant slowly and softly, we gradually increase our volume and rhythm, building-up the energy to a peak and abruptly stopping it at this peak. You, in effect, build the power and pop it off! This chant is primarily used as a magical aid to build, focus and send energy to an outward target.

2. In a somewhat similar fashion we build up energy, but instead of stopping the chant at the

peak, we recede back down to the original soft level, fading into an ending or building-up energy again as many times we desire. This is particularly good for power building in group use. Each time we peak and recede, everyone draws the energy into themselves, increasing their own personal energy reserves. This method can be combined with the first by building and lowering as many times as you wish, with the final surge popped off at the end.

3. This last method is a steady, repetitious, droning chant. The purpose is to facilitate a group trance. It is not meant to create a powerful push of energy, but to join the participants in a common focus and to create a trance state for the entire group. This is very effective as a bonding technique and in healing rituals. What is critical for the success of this is for the participants to "get out of their head-space" and get fully into the chant. Until this is accomplished—no trance state exists. This may happen in a short period of time or it may take a long while—the quality of time has a tendency to disappear when successful. Once the ecstatic state is achieved, one feels totally connected to the Source.

So, when do you use chanting in a ritual? For anything! Here are just a few examples where you can use chant:

- Circle casting

- Invocation of the elements

- Invocation of deity

- Power building for magical workings

- Energy building for healing work

- Group bonding

- Group play

- Feasting

- Releasing

- And whatever else you can think of!

What can *you* add to this list?

Some of the best rituals I have ever participated in were done entirely with chanting and dancing. Never a word was ever spoken.

Some rituals have words, but during the whole ritual while the spoken words are being said, those not speaking keep the energy up by softly humming. At no point in the ritual is the energy that's created by the singing voice allowed to die.

Have fun with singing and chanting! Be inspired to create your own chant. Remember the KISS principle and remember to make it fun! Find innovative ways to create group energy with chants and song!

Collecting Women

What I am able to do, seemingly without effort, is collect women. I use this phrase "collect women" to refer to the gathering and collecting of Goddess Women for the purpose of sharing their stories, exploring their divinity, having fun together and honoring the seasons and cycles of the year.

I say "without effort" but that is not entirely accurate! It does take dedication and the willingness to hang in there long enough to make it happen and also to see it through as it all comes together.

You want to find other women in your area. You want to get together with them and explore. What is it, though, that you really want to do? Do you want to study with others? Do you want to play with others? Do you want to have ritual? Do you want to make friends? There are so many ways to join with women! I learned a long time ago that if I want to find women I enjoy being with, I need to do it through activities I enjoy.

I have used the resources of the internet to find women for years. We have so much available to us. Putting the internet to work... works! Go to Yahoo Groups and look for Goddess Groups. Use the internet to look for organizations and groups for women whose focus is Goddess Spirituality.

E-lists are plentiful and if you cannot find exactly what you want, you can start one of your own! Once you have it created, it takes some getting-the-word-out, staying with the list to keep the threads going, and offering information and responses along the way—all of which encourage women to speak and interact.

You may also want to explore your local Unitarian Universalist Church. They are very open to women who honor the Goddess.

Take yourself wherever women gather. Be willing to be open. Be willing to speak freely (if you feel safe) about yourself and what you want. Hang out at local pagan shops, health food stores, or natural food places. Leave a card. Leave a flyer. Attend any event you can find. Go to classes. Drop your shyness and talk! Do not be afraid to say who you are, how you feel, or what you have experienced. Share your experience, strength, and hopes, and others will respond. Believe me, there are others looking for exactly what you are!

I am a priestess. I mentor other women who feel called to priestess for the Goddess. As a high priestess, I formed my own Tradition from the Traditions I hived off from. Each is lovely. However, staying within them limited my desire to explore beyond. I created The Apple Branch to speak to that need. It is through this Tradition that I teach, share and guide women who also wish to be priestesses. When a woman decides to dedicate herself to the work of the Goddess, she is a priestess. My job is to help them find their skills, develop new ones, and help them come into their own fullness. A certain amount of my collecting of women is dedicated to this purpose.

It has been my experience that women think there are only two ways to bring Goddess Women together, through either a study group or by starting their own circle. There are so many other ways to come together. Nothing stands in the way of creating what you want, except a limited imagination.

I love to sing, and I like to bring women together to sing to develop harmonies, rejoice in the gift of music, and sing Her praises.

I enjoy "crafty" things, and I like to collect women to work with their hands, the way women always have, in shades of quilting and sewing circles—much like when farmwomen came together to shell freshly harvested peas and beans; they would sit together and share their stories. And through the sharing of stories women continue to learn and grow strong together.

I love to dance, and I like to bring women together to dance ecstatically, creating dances to honor goddesses, and dancing with masks and costumes.

It takes a bit of imagination, it takes a lot of work, but it brings joy beyond measure! The methods for doing it are the same in every case—networking, talking, and spreading the word. Decide what you want and go for it. These are the things that give me joy, but you may have other things of your own. How about social

action, women's rights, the environment, herbalism, gardening, and drumming circles?
See? Look to your own imagination. It will be your work—find your joy in where you place your energies.

The secret lies in being willing, once you have started, once you have put the word out, to take on the load when it comes, even if at first you are the only one working to make it happen. If you can hang in there, you'll make it work. Then, the load can be spread out among those who find joy in being there also. It does not take much experience. It does not take a lot of knowledge. It takes honesty, a desire to share, and a willingness to work to make it happen. But most of all it takes enthusiasm and joy!

When you offer your work up as a service to the Goddess and Her Women, every bit of it, and all of the energy you put forth, will bring three-fold rewards unto your life. When it comes to the lives of the women you touch, well, you will feel so blessed by the experience of finding them, knowing them, and loving them, that you will wonder what you had been waiting for!

Feminism, Politics, and Spirituality

"Feminism has fought no wars. It has killed no opponents.
It has set up no concentration camps, starved no enemies, and practiced no cruelties. Its battles have been for education, for the vote, for better working conditions...for safety on the streets...for child care, for social welfare...for rape crisis centers, women's refuges, reforms in the law. If someone says, 'Oh, I'm not a feminist,' I ask, 'Why? What's your problem?'"

~Dale Spender, For the Record: The Making & Meaning of Feminist Knowledge, 1985

I don't believe there is any way to be involved in honoring and loving Goddess without being, in some way, involved in political action and or participating in trying to end oppression (my definition of feminism). I will grant that there will be varying levels of involvement among individuals, and certainly, that involvement waxes and wanes throughout our busy lives. But our consciousness is always present in these activities in some way.

We come to Goddess because we have been searching for new and better ways to live in our world. We all have come to agree with the old statement that *if you are not part of the solution, you are part of the problem*. Those of us who do want a better world have also learned that, in order for that to happen, we must be what we dream of being. And if we cannot fully achieve this yet, we should at least give it whatever we can until we get there.

There are women all over the world who participate in political actions. They stage events, sit down for peace, march and rally, write letters, and campaign for candidates who represent their views. All are working hard for a better world. We have people in positions of power, people who vote in ways that are not in keeping with our beliefs because a minority of voters elected our government officials. It is sad when less than half of the eligible voters actually vote. Certainly we do not have officials elected by a majority. We have a silent majority. It is our responsibility to know who our candidates are and do whatever we can to be represented by those who hold a healing, life-affirming worldview.

We also work very hard to end oppression of all kinds. It used to be that feminism was about women's rights, but no longer. Feminism is now about bringing the concepts of a more equal, egalitarian way of living into our world, where all are valued, each is given equal space, an equal voice, and equal opportunity to enjoy the abundance that life has to offer. This cannot happen until each of us examines our own prejudices, entitlements, and ways of interacting with others, including both privileged and oppressed peoples. Then we work on those values, adjusting our actions and ways of living in the world. And finally, we take that newfound awareness out into the world and ally ourselves with those who are oppressed, working with them as brothers and sisters to end the vicious cycle of oppression.

Become informed. Know who your local politicians are. Know your senators, congressional representative, and your mayor. Participate as a knowledgeable voter. Then vote. Encourage others to become informed. Encourage others to vote. Help them get to the polls if you can!

Learn even more about oppression. Read books by Bell Hooks such as *Feminism is for Everybody!* Also try to look within yourself, see whether the values you were raised with can be considered those of the privileged or those of the oppressed in application. Strive to undo programming and any cultural conditioning you may find. Find your "hot spots." Get involved where your passion lies. Become an ally to a group of those less privileged and/or oppressed. Learn what being an ally means and how to be one effectively.

And finally, consider, how do you relate to our Mother Earth? On a scorecard, how would you grade yourself in the measures you have taken personally to be in harmony with Her, in recycling efforts both at home and at work, by selecting products for your home that are not harmful to Her, and by being a voice and a helping hand in getting others in on this work?

We all have so much work to do. By starting now, we are all making a difference, one witch at a time.

What to Do About Bullies

I could probably go on and on about this topic, so in the interest of education I offer the following information gathered in my own recovery. Why would I write about bullying at all? Are we not Goddess lovers, one and all? How would such behavior ever enter into a spiritual path that believes all life is sacred?

Well, we all come to this path with all of our old baggage. That baggage may include jealousy, fear, and a desire for the wrong kind of power, that which attempts to control others.

Bullying is not merely, as many belittle, an occasional stinging comment made by a significant other at the breakfast table, a bad day with the boss, or children wrestling on the playground.

Bullying is cruelty deliberately aimed at others with the intent of gaining power by inflicting psychological and/or physical pain.

Bullying behaviors are varied: name calling, humiliation, spreading rumors, gossiping, public ridicule, scape-goating or blaming, isolating, assigning poor work conditions and job assignments, or denying holiday and vacation time in the workplace, or more obvious punching, hitting, kicking, taunting, ostracizing, sexualizing or making ethnic or gender slurs, etc.

Those who are the targets of bullying often feel intense vulnerability, fear and shame, and increasingly lower self-esteem that may increase their likelihood of continued victimization. Victims may become depressed and feel powerless. Many who have been bullied over a long period of time become suicidal. Others may retaliate in acts of violence or begin to bully others.

Unfortunately for victims, many people who are sought out for support dismiss bullying by saying, "It's happened to all of us, just ignore it". Some will even say the victim must deserve it! For too many, bullying has become such a part of the fabric of everyday life that many look the other way, and many have become numb to its devastating effects. Others actually see bullying behaviors, yet they avoid intervening because they feel powerless to stop it.

Studies indicate that two-thirds of the attackers in thirty-seven different school shootings felt persecuted into doing so due to long histories of being bullied by classmates. Being the target of bullying is a major factor in youth suicide, and millions of Americans face abuse in the workplace on a daily basis.

Many bullies have been perfecting their skills of intimidation since early childhood. Without intervention, the feelings and beliefs of childhood bullies become strengthened and ingrained. Bullying on the playground is frequently only the beginning of a life pattern that culminates in domestic violence and/or bullying in the workplace. Bullies depend upon the confusion, fear or feelings of powerlessness in their intended victims, as well as the silence of those witnessing abuse, in order to continue their behaviors.

We learned through many interviews that those who had been life-long bullies continued to be so until someone had the courage to intervene. Bullies seem only to be temporarily empowered, and both bullies and their victims are injured by the helplessness, apathy and silence of others. We need to create workplace, school and community norms where aggression towards others is unacceptable, not because of strict law-enforcement or severe punishments, but simply because we care about one another.

Courage does not mean that we are without fear, it means, as Pee Wee Reese demonstrated in 1947, that we do not let our fears stop us from taking action:

"It is not death or pain or loss that robs us of power: It is the fear of death, the fear of pain, the fear of
loss that turns the manipulated into victimsand the manipulators into terrorists". (Abdullah, 1995, p. 56)

According to *Bullies* by Jane Middleton-Moz & Mary Lee Zawadski, "Bullying is frequent and systematic cruelty deliberately aimed at a person by a person or persons with the intent of gaining power over another by regularly inflicting psychological and/or physical pain."

The first chapter in this book is entitled *"Moving Out of Denial"*. This is a critical step. Bullies too often get away with bullying because we turn our backs, we do nothing to stop them, we don't stand beside the one being bullied, and we "don't want to get involved" because we are afraid it will happen to us.

Every day in America over 160,000 children miss school because of fears of bullying. About 20% of high school students who were surveyed said they had seriously considered suicide because of having been bullied. And, about 43% of our school children are afraid to go to the bathroom for fear of being bullied in the school restrooms.

Bullying exists in our schools, in relationships (both straight and gay), in the workplace, and anywhere there are people. And yes, pagans are no different.

It is vital that this national problem be addressed, and it begins with each individual. It begins with education and it begins by standing up and saying "NO!" When we see a sister or brother being bullied, we need to use our power to stand beside her/him, to let her/him know she/he is not alone. We cannot continue to be blind to it. We cannot be silent.

There are many excellent books on bullying that you can buy in a store or online. Here are some that I personally recommend:

Take the Bully by the Horns by Sam Horn

Bullies: Strategies for Survival by Jane Middleton-Moz and Mary Lee Zawadski

Woman's Inhumanity to Woman by Phyllis Chesler

How to Handle Bullies, Teasers, and Other Meanies by Kate Cohen-Posey

Odd Girl Out by Rachel Simmons
Reviving Ophelia by Mary Pipher

Books that are particularly useful for recovering from abuse:

The Gentle Art of Verbal Self-Defense by Suzette Hadin Elgin

The Gentle Art of Verbal Self-Defense at Work by Suzette Hadin Elgin

Tongue Fu by Sam Horn

How to Disagree Without Being Disagreeable by Suzette Haden Elgin

The Pagan Bully Website
http://www.geocities.com/pagan_bullies

Healing the Wounds

Each of us comes to adulthood wounded one way or another. We have either grown up with less-than-perfect parents (I'm not sure there's really any such thing as a perfect parent), or we had all the love and nurturing in the world. In either case our schools and our peers inflict injuries upon us as we mature. None of us can ever be immune to feeling hurts and injustices, or to being oppressed in some way or another.

This applies as we travel through life as adults as well. No matter how "schooled" we are, trained to reflect, take in and release those hurtful experiences we encounter, all of us acquire wounds. So really, it is a matter of degree, how wounded we are. Many reach adulthood, having never been children. Many others reach adulthood so hurt that all emotions are bottled up, sealed off and removed from conscious, everyday expression. We all grow up feeling powerless in many areas of our lives. And unless we learn how to release and let go of old traumas, we will perpetuate the injuries upon ourselves and others.

Finding real happiness and contentment in our lives is dependent on how well we learn about ourselves—what motivates us, what frightens us, what helps us move beyond fear and trauma, what gives us joy, what uplifts us, and what brings us love? We can never achieve all that we are meant to be in this life unless we embrace, and love, all of who we are.

Much of our work then, as we come to know ourselves on our spiritual journey, is about meeting face-to-face those old wounds, and calling up memories that still cripple us in their intensity. That is why I encourage my students to take it easy. Move slowly, learning and absorbing, assimilating and processing, for that dark shadow within us will come forward to reveal itself when ready. And blessed be that it will! It is my guess that much of that trauma, much of that hurt we experienced that has molded and shaped who we are today, is often the fuel behind our actions and accomplishments. While the initial injury was not a good thing, our resulting actions fueled by it, often become the catalysts for greatness!

I am not a therapist, so I cannot take you by the hand and lead you through your hurts, nor can I take you through the tunnel of darkness that may await you. I can share with you, though, some ideas to explore as you travel.

The Goddess has many, many faces and some of her faces appear to us as dark. They can be very frightening, as can their attributed stories be. These are the Goddesses who will take your into the dark and out again. It is in their stories that you will find direction. It is in their stories that you will find yourself. And it is in their stories that you will discover joyful release and embodied wisdom. Kali who dances with us in the darkness of death, Hecate who greets us at the Crossroads, Lilith who embraces us through sexual healing, and Medusa who helps us reclaim our power as women—I urge you to explore these incredible Goddesses who are so much a part of you.

Do take time to be still. Enter the stillness of life—become fully present and aware of all that is happening in the moment. Attune your awareness by using silence. The silence will open vistas to the subtleties of life. Embrace a regular meditation practice, journal with a passion, and walk in nature where it feels as though no one else has walked before. Observe the trees, talk to the plants along the way, watch the birds, and listen to the frogs. There is so much to experience, so much there for us, all connected, all related, our brothers and sisters, kin and family.

And finally, learn the art of sacred play. Discover in your everyday life and in your ritual work, with others or by yourself, the child who delights in small wonders. When was the last time you played jacks or jumped rope? When did you last play hopscotch or even ride a bike? Have you ever had anyone paint your entire body; decorate you with goddess symbols? Have you ever tried on a toe-ring, tried to belly dance, played a drum, or just skipped down the lane with a happy heart?

I invite you to engage in sacred play. Join with other women in your play if you can. Share your stories. Listen to each other without judgment or criticism, without trying to "fix" anything. Open your heart, listen with compassion, and know that there are others who will do the same for you.

Discover that every act in life is sacred, if you are open to it. Your shower each morning is a clearing-away of the old, the past. Try a salt scrub!

As a regular part of meal preparation, imbue your food with energy. Sing mantras into it as you cook. Bless and thank all that has sacrificed itself for the nourishment of your body.

Take time each day to share your gratitude. Give thanks for those friends, family, and events in your life, for all that brings you joy.

Create altars in your home, in your garden, and out along the path as you walk.

Learn healing skills and share those skills with others.

Practice bringing one small bit of joy each day to someone else.

Be all that you can be. Open yourself to the divine soul that you really are.

Walk hand-in-hand with Goddess.

Write poetry and sing Her Many Names. Dance with Her. Make love with Her...

Appendix

Here is a lot of information to help you get started in magical work, that is, until you learn (as a friend once shared with me) that it is ok to "color outside the lines."

Colors

Each color carries its own vibration, and since it is this vibration with which you will be working, the first step is to select a color that best suits your magical work. The following is a list of colors and the vibrations they produce:

RED	**ORANGE**	**YELLOW**
Strength	Encouragement	Persuasion
Health	Adaptability	Charm
Vigor	Stimulation	Confidence
Sexual passion	Attraction	Joy
Danger	Plenty	Comfort
Charity	Kindness	Clarity
Passion	Energy	Wisdom
Initiating	Removes fears	Reason
Movement	Self-confidence	Freedom
Activity	Movement	Intellect
Anger		

GREEN
Finance
Fertility
Luck
Energy
Growth
Fertility
Abundance
Prosperity
Balance
Renewal

BLUE
Tranquility
Understanding
Patience
Health
Truth
Devotion
Sincerity
Joy
Spiritual Upliftment
Peace

PURPLE
Tension
Power
Sadness
Piety
Sentimentality
Spirituality
Awareness
Honor
Motivation

WHITE
Cleansing
Purity
Reflects & mirrors
Contains all colors
Spiritual strength

BLACK
Absorbs all colors
Draws negativity
Cleansing

BROWN
Grounding
Harmony
Steadiness
Concentration

PINK
Love
Cooperation
Understanding
Softens belief systems
Success
Diplomacy
Unselfishness

GOLD
Solar power
Strength
Healing
Abundance
Prosperity
Success

SILVER
Lunar energy
Intuitive
Healing

Oils

The following oils are offered just to stimulate your imagination. They can be used for dressing your candle if using tapers or by adding a few drops to a jar candle. The oil contains plant helpers who are willing aids to your work. Oils can also be added to ritual hand-washing water, and used to anoint one's self and others. I even sometimes add oil to the incense I make.

ACACIA	Psychic development and abilities.
APPLE BLOSSOM	Brings happiness. Promotes lightheartedness.
APRICOT	Encourages new ideas.
BLESSING	Blessing and purifying.
CARNATION	Gives energy. Purifies.
CHERRY BLOSSOM	Peace, harmony, happiness, cheerfulness.
CYPRESS	Spirituality. Brings special blessings.
EUCALYPTUS	Healing in general, colds, flu, asthma, bronchitis, and any type of sinus problems.
FRANGIPANI	Attracts the opposite sex. Extremely magnetizing.

FRANKINCENSE	Freedom, truth, wisdom, mind clearing, calmness, honors, independence, dignity, progress, motivation, receptivity, spiritual growth and spirituality. Purifies.
GARDENIA	Carries the vibration of the warmer emotions such as love, understanding, calmness, peace and tranquility.
HONEYSUCKLE	Mind clearing and building. Study, intuition, self-control, receptivity, organization, adaptability, vitality, success, definite, sure, concentration, telepathy, unhesitating.
IRIS	Determination, mind-building, independence, concentration.
JASMINE	Spiritual love, raising vibrations. Protection, affection, clean-living, femininity, unselfishness, truth.
JOHN THE CONQUEROR:	Success and protection. Repels black magic, negativity, adverse conditions and sadness.

LAVENDER	Purifying, relaxing, energy building, peacefulness. Helps the broken-hearted.
LILAC	Peace, harmony, study, memory, concentration, mind clearing, understanding.
MAGNOLIA	Purity, clear thinking, love.
MUSK	Enhances the personality, determination and will power.
MYRRH	Spiritual. Repels evil, adversity, black magic, negativity, sadness, etc.
ORANGE BLOSSOM	Magnetic, attraction, compelling, success, activity, creativity, inspiration, cheerfulness, persuasion.
PATCHOULI	Fertility, love, lust. Also enhances peaceful separation, calming.
ROSE	Harmony, peace, calmness, love.
ROSE-GERANIUM	Protection. Removes sadness and fear.
ROSEMARY	Protection against evil, negativity, etc. Builds strength of character, self-assurance, good common sense, courage, determination, will-power.

SANDALWOOD	Promotes psychic abilities, telepathic power, astral travel, prophetic dreams, spirit communication, insight, foresight, etc.
SWEET PEA	Attracts love. Magnetic, compelling, drawing, loyalty, devotion.
VIOLET	Healing. Reunion
WISTERIA	Evokes the aid of the higher spiritual forces.
YLANG-YLANG	Attraction, success, protection from physical harm and psychic attack.

Planetary Associations

Examples of Astrological Associations and Suggested Corresponding Oils

ARIES	Red candle, gardenia oil.
TAURUS	Green candle, iris oil.
GEMINI	Orange candle, honeysuckle oil.
CANCER	Blue candle, rose oil.
LEO	Gold candle, orange blossom oil.
VIRGO	White candle, sweet pea oil.
LIBRA	Green candle, honeysuckle oil.
SCORPIO	Red candle, cypress oil.

SAGITTARIUS	Dark blue candle, musk oil
CAPRICORN	Brown candle, magnolia oil.
AQUARIUS	Purple candle, apricot oil.
PISCES	Blue candle, jasmine oil.

Planetary Influences

JUPITER	Represents peace of mind, serenity, buying and selling, health. Attracts money, material things; attracts and builds friendships, honors.
MARS	To gain courage, self-assurance, win lawsuits, preserve oneself and survive adversity, obtain military honors, cause separation and hostility.
MERCURY	Prophesying, communication, divination. Pertains to all matters of the intellect; study, concentration, telepathy, psychic development, acquire understanding, gaining knowledge, opening closed doors.

MOON	Protection in all ways, travel in safety, to acquire material possessions, prophetic dreams, reconciliation's, and any situations pertaining to children.
SATURN	Influences others, business and financial success, develops psychic ability.
SUN	Honors and finances, power over those in authority, spiritual growth, development and enlightenment, peace, harmony, friendships, new acquaintances, hope, inspiration, love.
VENUS	Inner and outer beauty, tranquility, love, friendships, sex, fertility, conception, happiness, kindness, creativity, understanding, warmth, truth, sincerity.

Moon Phases

NEW MOON   That very first sliver of light just peeking out. Excellent time for beginnings.

WAXING MOONS   (The time between the New Moon and the Full Moon). This is the time to beginning things, for creation and manifesting new areas of growth. Burn any candles pertaining to uplifting, attraction, magnetizing, increasing, uniting or re-uniting, restoring, improving, beginning, etc.

FULL MOON   This is when the Moon is at full power. Use the light of this moon for the raising the strongest energy. Burn candles pertaining to health and power.

                        The time between the Full

WANING MOON   Moon and the Dark Moon). This is the time to do magic for releasing. Letting Go. Burn candles pertaining to negativity.

DARK MOON   (The three days before the New Moon). I find this the very best time for removing obstacles and releasing those things no longer useful to us. And the night just before the first sliver of the new moon appears is excellent to begin manifesting work.

Days of the Week

For best results, burn candles on the day that is best suited to your astrological sign.

SUNDAY	Leo
MONDAY	Cancer
TUESDAY	Aries and Scorpio
WEDNESDAY	Virgo and Gemini
THURSDAY	Sagittarius and Pisces
FRIDAY	Libra and Taurus
SATURDAY	Capricorn and Aquarius

Seven Major Chakras of the Body

First Chakra
Location	Root, Vagina, Anus, Base of Spine
Color	Red
Element	Earth
Function	Survival
Sense	Smell

Second Chakra
Location	Sex Organs - Uterus, Ovaries
Color	Orange
Element	Water
Function	Sex, Pleasure, Creativity
Sense	Taste

Third Chakra
Location	Solar Plexus - Stomach, Kidneys, Intestines
Color	Yellow
Element	Fire
Function	Power, will
Sense	Sight

Fourth Chakra
Location	Heart - Heart, Lungs, Breasts
Color	Green
Element	Air
Function	Love
Sense	Touch

Fifth Chakra
Location	Throat - Throat, Lymph nodes, Tonsils
Color	Blue
Element	Spirit
Function	Communication
Sense	Hearing

Sixth Chakra
Location	Third Eye - Between brows
Color	Indigo
Element	Light
Function	Intuition
Sense	Sixth Sense, psychic

Seventh Chakra
Location	Crown of Head - Center top
Color	Violet
Element	Thought
Function	Enlightenment
Sense	Understanding

Suggested Reading

Author	Title	Subject
Andrews, Ted	Animal Speak	Animal Powers
Andrews, Ted	Animal-Wise	Animal Powers
March & McEvers	Only Way to Learn Astrology	Astrology
Anodea, Judith	Wheels of Life	Chakra
Hooks, Bell*	Feminism is for Everybody	Feminism
Eisler, Riane	Chalice and the Blade	General - Anthropological
Gimbutas, Marija	Goddesses and Gods of Old Europe	General - Anthropological
Gimbutas, Marija	Language of the Goddess	General - Anthropological
Neumann, Erich	Great Mother	General - Anthropological
Krupp, E	Beyond the Blue Horizon	General - Astronomy
Krupp, E	Echoes of the Ancient Skies	General - Astronomy
Hope, Murray	Psychology of Ritual	General - Ritual
Harrow, Judy	Spiritual Mentoring	General - Spiritual
Teish, Luisah	Carnival of the Spirit	General - Witchcraft & Voudon
Teish, Luisah	Jambalaya	General - Witchcraft & Voudon
Budapest, Z	Holy Book of Women's Mysteries	Goddess
Cunningham, Nancy	I Am Woman By Rite	Goddess
George, Demetra	Finding Our Way Through the Dark	Goddess

Author	Title	Category
George, Demetra	Mysteries of the Dark Moon	Goddess
Harding, Esther	Women's Mysteries (O/P)	Goddess
Monaghan, Patricia	Goddess Companion	Goddess
Monaghan, Patricia	Goddess Path	Goddess
Monaghan, Patricia	O Mother Sun	Goddess
Mountainwater, Shekhinah	Ariadne's Thread	Goddess
Starck, Marcia	Dark Goddess	Goddess
Starhawk	Dreaming the Dark	Goddess
Starhawk	Spiral Dance	Goddess
Starhawk	Truth or Dare	Goddess
Stein, Diane	Women's Spirituality Book	Goddess
Stepanich, Kisma	An Act of Woman Power	Goddess
Noble, Vicki	Double Goddess	Goddess - Anthropology
Noble, Vicki*	Shakti Woman	Goddess - Anthropology
Redmond, Layne	When the Drummers Were Women	Goddess - Anthropology
Walker, Barbara*	Crone	Goddess - Anthropology
Spretnak, Charlene	Lost Goddess of Early Greece	Goddess - Myth
Stone, Merlin	Ancient Mirrors of Womanhood	Goddess - Myth
Stone, Merlin	When God Was a Woman	Goddess - Myth
Wilshire, Donna	Virgin Mother Crone	Goddess - Myth
Budapest, Z	Grandmother Moon	Goddess - Wheel of the Year

Author	Title	Category
Budapest, Z	Grandmother of Time	Goddess - Wheel of the Year
Eden, Donna	Energy Medicine	Healing
Stein, Diane	Essential Reiki	Healing
Stein, Diane	Natural Remedy Book	Healing
Stein, Diane	Woman's Book of Healing	Healing
Cunningham, Scott	Encyclopedia of Magical Herbs	Herbs
Baldwin, Christina	Life's Companion	Journaling
Ashcroft-Nowicki, Dolores	Magical Thought Forms	Magical Theory
Foux, Jan de	Amergin	Mythology
Ashcroft-Nowicki, Dolores	Highways of the Mind	Path working
Chesler, Phyllis	Woman's Inhumanity to Woman	Personal Development
Markova, Dawna	Open Mind	Personal Development
Rosenberg, Marshall	Nonviolent Communication	Personal Development
Imel, Dorothy	Goddesses in World Mythology	Reference
Monaghan, Patricia	Book of Goddesses and Heroines	Reference
Walker, Barbara	Women's Enc. of Myths and Secrets	Reference
Gitlin-Emmer, Susan	Lady of the Northern Light	Runes
Gitlin-Emmer, Susan	Runes, A Woman's Guide	Runes
Thorsson, Edred	Futhark	Runes
Marks, Kate	Circle of Song	Songs & Chants
Middleton, Julie	Songs for Earthlings	Songs & Chants

Forrest		
Melody	Love is in the Earth	Stones
Simmons, Robert & Ashain, Naisha	The Book of Stones	Stones
Cunningham, Scott	Enc. of Crystals, Gems and Metals	Stones

Bibliography

Judith, Anodea, *Wheels of Life*, St. Paul, MN, Llewellyn Publications, 1988

Cunningham, Scott, *Encyclopedia of Magical Herbs*, St. Paul, MN, Llewellyn Publications, 1988

Monaghan, Patricia, *Book of Goddesses and Heroines*, St. Paul, MN, Llewellyn, 1990

Spender, Dale, *For the Record: The Making & Meaning of Feminist Knowledge*, New York, NY, Pantheon, 1985

Wolfe, Amber, *In the Shadow of the Shaman*, St. Paul, MN, Llewellyn Publications, 2004

Manufactured by Amazon.ca
Bolton, ON